The WHO at WINTERLAND, 1968 and 1976

TEENAGE WASTELAND

EDOARDO GENZOLINI
FOREWORD BY JOEL SELVIN

SCHIFFER PUBLISHING
4880 Lower Valley Road • Atglen, PA 19310

Other Schiffer books by the author

The Who: Concert Memories from the Classic Years, 1964 to 1976, 978-0-7643-6402-0

Cream: Clapton, Bruce & Baker Sitting on Top of the World: San Francisco, February–March 1968, 978-0-7643-6592-8

Other Schiffer books on related subjects

Fleetwood Mac in Chicago: The Legendary Chess Blues Session, January 4, 1969
Jeff Lowenthal and Robert Schaffner, 978-0-7643-6495-2

The Atlanta Rhythm Section: The Authorized History
Willie G. Moseley, 978-0-7643-5564-6

Photos on cover by Frank Stapleton and Dave Hori. Photos on endsheets courtesy of Dawn Hall Estate of Douglas Kent Hall (scans from original negatives preserved at Princeton University Library), and by Dave Hori. Negatives on back cover courtesy of Craig Patterson, items photo by Stefano Domenichetti Carlini. Winterland's billboard photo on inside back cover by Dennis McCoy, courtesy of whocollection.com.

Designed by Danielle D. Farmer
Cover design by Christopher Bower
Type set in Arbotek/Compacta Bd BT/Georgia Pro

ISBN: 978-0-7643-6735-9
Printed in China

Published by Schiffer Publishing, Ltd.
4880 Lower Valley Road
Atglen, PA 19310
Phone: (610) 593-1777; Fax: (610) 593-2002
Email: Info@schifferbooks.com
Web: www.schifferbooks.com

For our complete selection of fine books on this and related subjects, please visit our website at www.schifferbooks.com. You may also write for a free catalog.

Schiffer Publishing's titles are available at special discounts for bulk purchases for sales promotions or premiums. Special editions, including personalized covers, corporate imprints, and excerpts, can be created in large quantities for special needs. For more information, contact the publisher.

We are always looking for people to write books on new and related subjects. If you have an idea for a book, please contact us at proposals@schifferbooks.com.

DEDICATION

To every teenager who right now, in this moment,
lonely in his or her room, is discovering the Who.

EPIGRAPH

It hasn't been quite so long now
since the last time you flashed into my life
and once again we gather to feel your note
and let you soar into harmony with our own.
A room of souls
always searching for a way to be free
looking at you for an answer
and you are looking at us
trying to see who we really could be.
In the dark you come into our lives
and dance and clown around and around
bringing your crystal shining light
until you are gone—once again gone
leaving us with the dream of memories
to add to your legend.
We return home with you in our hearts
and more visions in our eyes.

SANSARA-NIRVANA MURPHY
March 27, 1976, 5:15 p.m.
Winterland, San Francisco, California

ONTENTS

FOREWORD

Paul Butterfield Blues Band at the Fillmore on January 20, 1967.
Ted Streshinsky Photographic Archive / Corbis Historical via Getty Images

The weekend the Who first came to play the Fillmore Auditorium, San Francisco sat in the middle of the pop music universe, citadel of an exciting new musical movement sweeping the globe. San Francisco's leading new band, Jefferson Airplane, was poised on the top of the bestselling charts with "Somebody to Love." The underground rock that had emerged from the acid-rock ballrooms of San Francisco over the previous eighteen months had spread around the country and across the Atlantic, but San Francisco was the remote fountainhead, the quaint little city on the edge of the Western world where LSD had ignited a vast cultural boogaloo.

The Monterey Pop Festival was taking place that weekend a couple of hours' drive south, a convergence of all the leaders of this new music from London, New York, Los Angeles, and, most significantly, San Francisco. These acid-drenched hippie rock groups had barely been seen outside their native environs. They were only beginning to release records—albums had appeared from San Francisco bands that year included Grateful Dead, Country Joe and the Fish, Moby Grape—and they performed only at San Francisco dance halls such as the Fillmore or Avalon Ballroom. The festival was gathering the leaders of this new music, and the Who were scheduled to play the festival's closing night on Sunday.

Other underground bands such as the Doors or Canned Heat from Los Angeles had made their way to play the San Francisco ballrooms. Even New York's dark and druggy Velvet Underground passed through the Fillmore, but San Francisco was the epicenter, and the Fillmore was the mother church. At this point, the very start of what was already being touted as the "Summer of Love," San Francisco rock was little more than a rumor, an urban legend, a secret society that had unlocked the mysteries of rock music known to few outside the immediate area.

The Who knew the Fillmore by reputation, although the same cannot be said for the audience at the Fillmore. Although the band was already widely recognized in their native Britain as one of the leading lights of new rock in England, America had not gotten the word yet. "Happy Jack" was the band's current single, getting modest to light airplay on the ubiquitous AM radio stations of the day, but in San Francisco there was yet another new wrinkle to contend with —underground radio.

A former foreign-language station called KMPX had converted to underground rock under the guidance of former Top 40 AM boss jock Tom "Big Daddy" Donahue. A grand collection of misfits, miscreants, and reprobates served as the station's air staff, and they roamed far and wide in the choices they made for records to play. It was free-form radio at its most free. The station had, for instance, picked up English copies of the debut album by the Jimi Hendrix Experience that would not be released in the States until the following August, and slammed every track on the album in the weeks prior to his US debut performance that weekend at the Monterey Pop Festival. He would play the Fillmore the following weekend as opening act for Jefferson Airplane, who left town the next morning after watching Hendrix wipe the floor with them the first night of the six-night engagement. Big Brother and the Holding Company, house band at the Avalon in their first Fillmore dates, substituted the rest of the week for the Airplane.

The Who were a delicacy offered on occasion on the KMPX menu, not a staple. The mini suite "A Quick One While He's Away" found a certain favor on the underground radio station, which tended to feature lengthy tracks that AM radio wouldn't dare touch, such as the Doors' "The End" or the full version of "Light My Fire," also currently popular on KMPX. The Who to San Francisco audiences at this point were an exotic treat from the distant mod culture of swinging London, hardly a main attraction. With most of the San Francisco mainstays playing Monterey that weekend, they topped a bill that also featured the Loading Zone, a Berkeley-based rhythm-and-blues band that was something of a minor fixture on the East Bay scene, and unbilled newcomers added to the show too late for the poster in the first of what would turn out to be many Fillmore performances, at this time called the Santana Blues Band. By the end of the next year, Santana would be drawing capacity crowds of their own to the Fillmore West long before they played their first out-of-town concert at Woodstock or recorded their first album.

The Who were devastating that first weekend at the Fillmore. They climaxed the band's opening set with "A Quick One . . ." They returned for a second set delivered with pure vengeance, crash landing with Moon erupting from behind the drums on "My Generation," as Townshend beat his guitar into submission on the Fillmore stage. The rank explosion of violence to bring the cataclysmic set to a finish left the stoned hippies in the hall slack-jawed and open mouthed. They were too stunned to applaud.

By the time the Who returned to San Francisco in February 1968, the rock music world had made quite a few revolutions around the sun. Underground rock was no longer the rare and precious thing it had been that summer weekend of the year before, but it was now the dominant sound of the day's pop music. Although the Who had still not broken through to a wide American audience, their supremacy as a live British rock band was fully recognized by the time the group returned for their second San Francisco engagement, returning to the Fillmore for the opening night and completing the three-night engagement at the larger Winterland, more than four times the size of the smaller hall. The San Francisco bands— Airplane, Dead, Big Brother with Janis Joplin, Quicksilver Messenger Service, Steve Miller Band—were at the vanguard of the new rock sound across the country, no longer relegated to regional seclusion. There were little Fillmores and booming FM underground radio stations in every city.

Bill Graham was no longer the proprietor of the sole dance hall, but an ambitious impresario planning to open a New York operation the next month called Fillmore East. In San Francisco, Graham was drawing crowds too large for the Fillmore, so he moved shows from the 1,100-seat ballroom on Thursday nights to the 5,400-capacity ice rink Winterland, two blocks away, for the weekend shows. He was also acting as manager of Jefferson Airplane, one of the nation's most popular rock bands. In February alone, he would bring to San Francisco concerts by Jimi Hendrix, Paul Butterfield Blues Band, Cream (who would record their live album *Wheels of Fire* that weekend at Winterland), and the Who. The golden age of rock had dawned.

It was the beginning of a long and rewarding relationship between the Who and their San Francisco constituency. Over the years, some of the band's most memorable performances would take place in San Francisco—the epic, overcrowded *Tommy* performance at Fillmore West in 1969; the massive show at Berkeley Community Theater in 1970; the unreal *Who's Next* concert at S.F. Civic in 1971; the catastrophic *Quadrophenia* tour opener at the Cow Palace in 1973, where drummer Keith Moon passed out twice before the band finished the set with a drummer drawn from the audience; one final pass through Winterland in 1976, one of the band's final live shows before Moon died.

San Francisco in the Summer of Love was where the Who first connected with American audiences. They spent the rest of the summer in dubious glory opening shows for teenybopper heroes Herman's Hermits. When they returned to San Francisco the following year, they were ready to meet American audiences on their own terms. In San Francisco, they discovered a dialogue with their audience that would sustain them through the band's trajectory.

Joel Selvin
San Francisco Chronicle pop music critic (1970–2009)

PREFACE

The book that you are holding is the result of an impossible experiment. Despite the many photos it shows and the many stories it tells, the main feature I invite you to consider, which I find essential, is the obsession that drove its making, which, for its nature, was not and won't ever be fulfilled. At first glance, it may look like a nostalgic operation to celebrate a context, a time, and a place—the Who in San Francisco in 1968 and 1976—which many of those who were there remember today indeed with particular fondness and nostalgia. But this project wanted to go beyond that. Its aim was to do away with nostalgia, by trying to eliminate the gap between the object and the person experiencing it. In other words, this book is the impossible challenge to defeat space and time, in order to reenact the time of a band hanging out and playing in a particular city on three particular days of February 1968 and on two particular days of March 1976. How can one do that? One, as just said, simply cannot. So, how can one at least *try* to do that? One way could be by combining as many accounts about the Who while in San Francisco in those days, in addition to not just displaying the best photographs that immortalize the four guys then and there, but displaying the *whole film rolls*, whenever available, and offering more than just one photographer's perspective. This is why you won't find only "good" shots here, but also those that would have been scrapped from other books. The main goal, in this sense, couldn't be farther from the intention of offering an "ideal" picture of a band in two specific moments in their career, but to depict it and that context as truthfully as possible.

Going through this book, my first impression is that it feels like attending silent concerts, but after all, silence is the sound of time, and it is particularly so if the time that is told, like it is in this book, is over. The end of that time has allowed, however, space to materialize itself. This volume is the result of a mad search of the scattered pieces of space that are left from that experience, particularly from Winterland.

Choosing Winterland over the more celebrated Fillmore Auditorium seems unusual, but it was in fact a conscious and sought-after choice derived from solid intentions; the bond of the Who with the city of San Francisco and that particular venue appears so tight that it looks like their destinies were weaved together. I found it particularly meaningful and symbolic, in this respect, that the passing of Keith Moon, on September 7,

1978, and the closing of Winterland, on December 31, 1978, are just a little more than three months apart. Also, Winterland was the only venue the Who played twice in San Francisco, after a considerable number of years between one date and the other (although Pete Townshend would return to the old Fillmore Auditorium on 1805 Geary Boulevard, twenty-eight years after his last time, for a solo concert on April 30, 1996); I found that the huge Winterland building could be the most faithful custodian of the Who's memory and identity, representing a time capsule revealing the beginning and the end of the band's career with Keith Moon.

Finally, the book's title; during one of the many conversations with my friend Mark d'Ercole, I told him I would have liked to call this book "Teenage Wasteland," at which point he burst out laughing: "You don't know what you just said! One time I was going to a Grateful Dead concert at Winterland, and when I got to the place, there was a line going around the block, with people laying on the ground, with their mouths agape . . . So, as I went around the corner and saw all these bodies, I thought, "Wow, so that's the teenage wasteland that Pete talked about!" Right then, I knew that was the perfect title for this book. However, as I originally saw it, the title really refers more to what the future holds than the past could ever do. After everything in this book is past and gone, this thing you are holding, this impossible experiment, will be the only thing that will be left to tell the story of a particular time and place. May this work survive until it's the only thing standing, like the monolith on the *Who's Next* cover, on the deserted ground that first generated it. To anyone who'll care to know, this book will remind them of what this ground used to look like a long time ago; anyone who'll care will learn it wasn't only a wasteland.

ONLY a teenage wasteland.

ACKNOWLEDGMENTS

This book wouldn't have been the same without the great help particularly of Sansara-Nirvana Murphy, Brad Rodgers (whocollection.com), and Princeton University Library. Sansara has trusted me and has believed in this project from the very beginning, letting me work directly on her original negatives, color slides, and two Super 8 films from Berkeley 1970 and Winterland 1976. I feel happy and honored to be able to show her mesmerizing work on the Who.

I am also thrilled to display the unique documentation made by Dennis McCoy prior to, during, and after the March 27, 1976, appearance of the Who at Winterland, for the first time in an unprecedented high quality and almost in its entirety. I thank Brad Rodgers very much for this, since he owns the copyright to Dennis's photos and allowed me to work directly on the original black-and-white negatives.

Also, Princeton University Library's service made the difference in this project by scanning and providing me with the full set of black-and-white photos by Douglas Kent Hall from Winterland, February 23, 1968, allowing the discovery of some of the best—and never seen before to this day—portraits of the Who from 1968. I warmly thank Dawn Hall of the Douglas Kent Hall Estate for making the connection with Princeton possible.

Much love and gratitude to old friends Craig Patterson (who took probably my favorite portrait ever of Pete while backstage at Winterland on February 24, 1968, receiving a Kay guitar as a gift), Mark d'Ercole, Nick Schram, Rich Martin Frost, Frank Stapleton, Paul Sommer, and John Peden, and to new friends Dan Davis, Shirley and Maria Streshinsky, Douglas P. Bratt, Tom Tallon, Eric Seedman, Shigeto Murase, Jarid S. Johnson, Dave Hori, and Adam Folkes; Adam's dad, Craig Folkes, was one of the great photographers in Los Angeles, and his shots of the Who at the Shrine Exposition Hall from June 1968 are just a little example of a much-wider work I hope to see published in the future in a book about him made by his family. I thank James Johnston for being the person from whom I first found out about Craig Folkes.

A heartfelt mention to those who participated in this work with their written contributions, stories, and information, or who suggested leads to new, fruitful connections or photographic sources; first of all, thanks to Joel Selvin: his books have always been the backbone of my knowledge about San Francisco, and I am, to say the least, honored to see my work introduced by his foreword.

Much gratitude to Rick Chapman, who runs the Meher Baba Information Center in Berkeley, and whose books about Baba helped me access a deeper understanding of Pete Townshend's compositions and lyrics. Thanks to Rick I have realized how Baba's words are an essential key, albeit often underestimated, to get through to Pete's world. I thank Raine Eastman-Gannett for making my connection with Rick possible.

Thank you also to legendary sound engineer Bill Halverson, and to Steven Novak, James Terry Leary, Mike Wiseman, Michael E. Tassone, Michael Lazarus Scott, the late JP Palmer, and Michael Weber for their precious anecdotes and stories. Thanks to Neal Izumi for making the connection with Dave Hori possible.

There are others that I'd like to thank but have decided to keep anonymous—you know who you are; similarly, I have found many more never-seen-before photos that, for uncertain copyright attribution and other different reasons, I could not display in this book. I hope I'll be able to show them in further printings.

A particular note about the reel-to-reel recording from the Fillmore and Winterland (February 22 and 23) I often mention in the text: this was originally made by Steve Cowley and then given to Tom Tallon, who lent it to Mark d'Ercole, who finally gave it to me in 2018.

A warm thank you to everyone at Schiffer Publishing, particularly my editor Bob Biondi, for believing in my projects from our first connection in 2020, and for helping me give my nerdy obsessions the best presentation I could ever wish for.

Eternal love to my family—Afra, Marco, Leonardo, and our cats Moka, Wendy, and Indiana (and Nemo, Tony, and Jones, present now more than ever). Thanks to my beautiful Chiara.

It may sound superfluous and obvious, but thanks to the Who; thank you, Pete, for being my greatest inspiration and guiding light since my teenage years.

INTRODUCTION

f we think of the Who, which years spontaneously stand out in our mind? Any moment in their career that our mind should pick out would automatically stand for what we consider to be the band's most representative, for different reasons. It would be an unconscious process based on our personal experience; for instance, the first Who album we heard, or the first time we saw the Who live. Both events would have had an indelible impact on our lives. It could as well be an unconscious reaction affected by general opinion, which indirectly dictates which identity of the Who, embodied by each of their albums, is or should be accepted as the band's finest. In this sense, we may think of 1965, with *My Generation*—the birth of the Who through their eponymous anthem. Or 1969, with *Tommy*; or, for many, *Tommy at* Woodstock—the event that gave the Who definitive world recognition, thanks also to the classic documentary by Michael Wadleigh, which came out in 1970. That contributed to identifying, for many, 1970 as the apex year of the band's career: in addition to appearing in the *Woodstock* film, the Who were immortalized onstage with *Live at Leeds*, crowned by the *New York Times* as the best live album ever recorded. Nevertheless, I am sure the majority of us would pick 1971: Life House, too great of a concept for just one album. But yet, look at what came out of it: *Who's Next*, one of the greatest albums of all times. Or why not 1973? *Quadrophenia*, the great mod epic . . .

What would emerge from a hypothetical survey such as this is that the career of the Who generally and statistically circles around the years in which great single albums and classic concept albums were made, automatically overlooking the moments in between, which only erroneously are often considered of minor importance. Years such as 1968 and 1976 are not those that one would generally think of when it comes to identifying the best incarnation of the Who. In particular, on one hand, 1968 sees the band caught in frustration for struggling to find a balance between artistic vocations and having to meet the record company's need for the band to become a smash-hits factory, churning out one album after the other; it is also the time with the poorer production of visual and audio documentation from concerts, if we consider the tight touring schedule and the staggering number of songs that were almost compulsively recorded in studio and released to desperately meet the label's tasks. On the other hand, 1976 sees the Who leaving behind the rock opera tradition, which had been carried throughout the seventies as a heavy and an almost deadly burden, and

returning to basics, with a new album released at the end of the previous year, *The Who by Numbers*, introducing (or getting back to) a new, essential and stripped-down outfit of band.

Choosing to juxtapose these two years might feel unusual, in that both depict the Who in two radically different identities—one of the pop art ballroom days, one of the stadium rock band—and in two radically different sociocultural contexts—the sixties and the seventies. The Who, within this comparison, almost look like two different bands, and, to some extent, they were. In such a sea of differences, maybe not the only but the most evident common factor that ties 1968 and 1976 together, crossing almost ten years, is the *live* dimension. In 1968, as much as in 1976, the touring factor strongly surpassed and transcended the mere promotional purpose and took on a higher, almost spiritual meaning. As we will see closely further on in the reading, the touring experience in those two particular years came to mean self-affirmation and rebirth for the Who. What is important to recognize is that it wasn't something meant to happen in any other circumstance and in any other geographical and sociocultural context: this almost spiritual experience is necessarily connected and consequent to the discovery of America for the Who, starting in the spring of 1967.

Up until then, the Who had notched up a series of Top 10 singles and had two albums behind them, *My Generation / The Who Sings My Generation* and *A Quick One / Happy Jack*, which, combined with incendiary live performances that shook London clubs' and theaters' walls, made them gain the reputation that was fated to inevitably stick to their skins for the next decades, facing myth, misunderstandings, free interpretation, and controversies, from being addressed as the epitome of mod band, to be recognized as the first example of punk . . . to the extent that we may even begin to feel that the "great rock-and-roll swindle" occurred one decade before the Sex Pistols in 1976, and it wasn't perpetrated by any band in particular, but by general opinion. What I am trying to say here is that this rock-and-roll swindle *ante litteram* saw the Who being widely and unfairly oversimplified throughout the years. For one thing, if there is any truth to them having been mods, then it was only conceptually, on an idealistic level, in their attitude of being so much "in the present" to be extremely self-aware and to make their act generally impervious to the standard comprehension's schemes. As Roger Daltrey confessed in 1975, the Who were too old to be mods:

In England, we had the Teddy Boys, which was the late '50s, who started wearing Edwardian clothes, really long draped jackets, really stovepipe trousers and big suede boots. And the mod thing was the first big cult thing to follow after that. And that was just like a general identity for kids, from the age of fifteen to eighteen. The Who at the time were all nineteen or twenty [laughs]. We were never mods . . . but the Who became the group which the mods really identified with. We played the music they liked. And we were their group.[1]

Fillmore West. 10 South Van Ness, San Francisco, California. Thursday, August 15, 1968. *Photo by Paul Sommer*

The general misunderstanding of the Who's act lies in the fact that the auto-destructive and thunderous side of their performance had underpinnings pertaining to aesthetics and avant-gardist references, coming from Pete's Art School studies, that are generally overlooked and were disregarded by the Who's posterity. The English punk bands, for instance, would take only the external, more recognizable features of the Who's act— the impetuous, violent, Sturm und Drang side of it that also appealed so much to mods in the early sixties— but stripped it down only to an impulsive, nihilistic, youthful wail; contrary to all the self-destructing implications to the Who's attitude that Pete's act inadvertently produced, the guitar smashing was perpetrated by Pete with the intent to produce an ecstatic, liberating effect. As Pete told John Gilliland in this respect in his *Pop Chronicles* radio program series, on February 5, 1968,

> The smashing is more the Who than other stuff. . . . It does us probably the most good, out of anything we do; it gives us the biggest kicks. . . . It's so fantastic just to do something so exhibitionist, so focusing, so traumatizing, melodramatic in front of so many people. It's got all the kind of the perversion of ripping off all your clothes, all the wonder of complete lack of inhibitions. . . . The abandon of it is the main thing, just complete freaking out; sometimes angrily, sometimes happily.[2]

This, as well as aiming to elude any materialistic feature in music, putting it across in its purest, its most immediate, and as multilayered form as possible:

> There is nothing between you and the music; there is nothing. At the end of the show there's still nothing between you and the music. There is nothing to stop you getting the ultimate sound out of the guitar, because you're not caring about the finishing of it; you're not in love with the thing. I'm not a guitar lover; I'm a guitar player. If you get to do a bad show, you smash up your guitar and [it] becomes a good show; if you do a good show, you smash your guitar and [it] becomes even a better show! It's a finale, it's the ultimate finale—you get to the point where you literally can't play another note, because there's nothing to play it on. The show's over, folks.[3]

Pete Townshend saw in pop music the *milieu* through which to carry out his artistic operation: as he told BBC director Tony Palmer in March 1968,

> If you look at *any* form of art, you can find something in the best of pop which completely eliminates the old form. If you think that Mahler's "Ninth Symphony" is overwhelming, I can play you a tape which I made in my studio which is *more* overwhelming. Benjamin Britten, for example, is hung up on Purcell. So am I, but I think *I* was getting nearer to what Purcell was getting at musically in my song "I'm a Boy" than Benjamin Britten was in the whole of his work.[4]

After all, as Townshend would admit, the only one to blame for the misunderstanding of the Who's music is the *talk about music* itself, which becomes inevitable at some point. Pop is its own victim.

"I have to admit," continues Pete, "that I find it very difficult to talk about pop music, since to start with there isn't such a thing as 'pop' music. There are many different kinds of music all called 'pop.' You can't say that the sounds I produce are the same as those of Donald Peers. They're totally different—but they're both called 'pop.' For me, my kind of pop is being the leader of youth; it's being in the present. But the more you talk about that, the more confused you become; the best thing is not to be talking but to pick up a guitar and be playing it. Because that's what pop music is really about. Pop music isn't me sitting reasoning out its role; it's me picking up a guitar and playing you a song. After all, even to go bang, bang on a guitar does get a lot of things said—although *you* may not like what is being expressed. Pop music is ultimately a show, a circus. You've got to hit the audience with it. Punch them in the stomach and kick them on the floor. Pop music will cease to be [of] any interest if it gets too interested in musical or lyrical obscurity, because when it comes down to it, its purpose and its value is in the creation of an immediate and overwhelming excitement."[5]

Pete went deeper into the theoretical references behind the gear's destruction at Tony Palmer's microphone in 1968, making his point. In this, Pete mentioned the German artist Gustav Metzger, who had a huge impact on him as a young student during art school:

I've written a thesis for Gustav Metzger—the auto destructive artist. I said that our audience is numbed by seeing violence in the same way that they're numbed by seeing a car crash. It's a traumatic experience. But it *does* release basic tensions—just like other people do when they fly off the handle. Lack of control and basic abandon are qualities that people don't particularly admire or respect in others; but at the same time, they don't seem to realize that they *themselves* have also got these things stuffed inside them. So, our performances and our music have got much more to do with art and life than people imagine. Much, much more to do with pop music than anything else.

His final statement is definitive:

We're not out to blow people's minds, however. We're out to get through to them.[6]

Pete would come back to the topic in June 1969:

The current big, imperishable, holy art is pop music, and the breakup routine really says something about it. The ideal, of course, would be for me to get killed in an airplane right after a stupendous performance.[7]

From Pete's words we can get a better idea of the sophisticated vision he had for his band, and how struggling must have been for him to lead the Who to a direction that could—he hoped—meet, at the same time, his artistic vocations and the necessary music business tasks in order to stay afloat.

This brings us to March 1967, when the Who headed for the conquest of the West.

THAT MOTHERLAND FEELING:

THE WHO'S FIRST TIME IN SAN FRANCISCO,

JUNE 1967

Chapter 1

Breaking the American market was the ultimate goal for English bands, in order to gain world recognition and not to be forgotten in the limbo of the hundred groups that had blossomed in the wake of the Beatles' success. England had proved a static reality, and London was a city that, as Roger Daltrey admitted in January 1968, "was and is only superficially swinging."[1] Being exposed to the American audiences was even more necessary for the Who, since Pete came to terms with the fact that the real essence of his band could emerge exclusively live: "It's important for us to perform in public. You really can't tell what we do by our records,"[2] not without nurturing some perplexities, doubt, and frustration, however: "The only drag is that unless we smash the gear up, we don't get in the public eye, particularly in a country as vast as America. We just have to do it if we want to make fame quickly. We just give people a big show—they can dig the sound on records later. We can't smash up guitars on records; they'll just have to listen to the songs. . . . We don't try to justify our bursting instruments, but it took us five years to make it in England. We don't want to spend another five making it in America."[3]

Nevertheless, Pete's apprehension would soon disappear: once in the States for the first time in March–April 1967, playing Murray the K's "Music in the Fifth Dimension" shows at RKO Theater in New York, Pete saw in the audience something different than what he was expecting to find: the days when bands used to fight with their feeble equipment against deafening decibels of screaming kids tearing their hair out seemed to have ended; now, audiences were actually *listening*.

As Pete remembered,

> What was happening at the Murray the K show, which should have been a lesson for the promoters to realize, was that the kids were coming in and they were staying *all* day. Because they liked the music. Not because they wanted to get away from school. They liked the music they were hearing and they wanted to hear it again and again and again.[4]

Hanging around the Haight–Ashbury neighborhood in 1967. *Courtesy of Dan W. Davis*

That first impression was soon to be confirmed when the Who arrived in San Francisco and played at Bill Graham's Fillmore Auditorium. The Who would never be the same after that, and thanks to the Fillmore experience, they started a path that led them to become the band we know today.

The Who arrived in San Francisco on June 16, 1967, when the city and the Bay Area was in its full swing and was going through a real "second cultural Renaissance,"[5] the "second great intellectual awakening in the USA," asserts Mike Wiseman, witness to that change taking place. "A whole lot of ideas were coming to fruition at that time," he adds. "We had Eastern spiritual philosophy being introduced on FM radio by Alan Watts; Black Power by Malcolm X on FM radio on Friday nights as well. In 1962, Mario Savio and some other UC Berkeley students started the free-speech movement, which then turned into the antiwar movement, not to mention all the scientific breakthroughs that were happening at that time. The world really did change, and the music had a part in that for sure."[6]

Music and psychedelics were a combination that constituted the underpinnings of a youth scene that had been flourishing in San Francisco since late 1965. Not to overlook the fact that the city swarmed with young people, thanks also to the low rents and free tuition to all public colleges and universities.[7] It really was a city of opportunities, and novice impresario Bill Graham found himself in the right time and place just like all the many others.

Bill was an orphan refugee who escaped the Nazi spread, which took him from Germany across Europe before finally settling in New York, in the Bronx. His acting vocation, mixed with his peculiar and natural entrepreneurial skills, took him to San Francisco, where he ended up managing the local mime troupe. His connection with the Fillmore Auditorium occurred through *San Francisco Chronicle* columnist Ralph J. Gleason, who pointed out the building to Bill as an ideal venue to stage the benefit events the San Francisco Mime Troupe was planning to organize on behalf of one of their members, Ronald Davis, who was arrested for obscenity during the re-presentation of the desecrating Giordano Bruno's play *The Candle Bearer* in Lafayette Park.

Fillmore Auditorium, located on 1805 Geary Boulevard, is often referred to as simply "the Fillmore" and affectionately as "the 'Old' Fillmore," as opposed to Bill's more "recent" Fillmore ballroom in San Francisco Fillmore West, opened in July 1968 inside the Carousel Ballroom building on 10 South Van Ness. The Fillmore was built in 1912 as the Majestic Dance Hall & Academy and went through many changes and managements before Bill Graham first stepped in in late 1965. At that time, the venue was being managed by promoter Charles Sullivan, the last representant of a scene that spread through the Fillmore district between the '40s and the '50s and gave the neighborhood the name "Harlem of the West" for the presence of many nightclubs frequented by Black clientele and where Black artists such as Etta James, Louis Armstrong, and Charlie Parker would perform. Sullivan gained the name "Mayor of the Fillmore" for being an eclectic cultural key figure in that area: in addition to presenting jazz and rhythm-and-blues acts at the Fillmore Auditorium, such as the Temptations and Little Richard, he lent money to local musician Slim Gaillard to open a club named Vout City, which was immortalized by Jack Kerouac in his novel *On the Road*.[8]

All this and more happened in the so-called Western Addition, an ethnic and cultural melting pot that gave the Bay Area an inclusive connotation.

In the early 1960s, with the jazz tradition progressively wearing away and giving way to rock and roll, San Francisco was going to face redevelopment plans that would redefine the physical and cultural landscape within a short time. With the risk that the Fillmore Auditorium could be affected by these drastic measures, Charles Sullivan decided to let the new generation of white promoters use his venue. Therefore, in December 1965, Bill Graham made two San Francisco Mime Troupe benefits at the Fillmore under Sullivan's concession and started to put on acts under his management together with the other historic local promoter, Chet Helms. The Helms-Graham relationship didn't last long because of the radically antithetical visions of the two of doing business, and soon Helms got swept away by Graham's Machiavellian attitude, for which the ends justify all means.

After Sullivan's sudden and still-mysterious death on August 1, 1966, Bill completely took over the Fillmore. He left the Mime Troupe, well aware of the lesson that the benefit initiatives taught him: those had an effect on the audience that was totally unexpected to Bill, and they lit a spark in his mind; he became aware of the receptiveness of the audience and took inspiration from the LSD-induced, mellowed-out, spontaneous surrounding music scene to conduct an extremely focused, rational operation. New York attitude meets San Francisco vibes: the music business that we know of today started right there, with the Fillmore as headquarters. Jerry Garcia, guitarist of the Grateful Dead, fondly remembered how Bill Graham collided with the peaceful music scene that blossomed from the Haight-Ashbury neighborhood, of which the Dead were probably the best representants, just like a meteor: "Bill was a *New Yorker*. A lot of us out here in California didn't have much experience with New Yorkers. It was like, 'Relax, man. *Slow down.*' He couldn't stand that shit. '*Mellow out.*' Oh, God. He'd go, '*Zaarrrh!*' It's that energy. He was the guy that taught us about that. A lot of us had never been out of California. You know, what else was going on anyplace else that you even wanted to know about? But to us . . . oh, boy. He was like a *Martian*."[9]

It is important to point out that what Bill was creating was deriving from his acute ability to observe, and the Fillmore worked as a repeater that captured the slightest signal and reverberated it throughout the country. Bill's operation inspired novice promoters to do their own thing: the best example is Russ Gibb with the legendary Grande Ballroom in Detroit, Michigan.

It is also important to observe that Bill did not conduct a sterile, ruthless, detached, money-making operation; what he did required both entrepreneurial skills but also a very deep sensitivity: Bill created extremely variegated lineups at the Fillmore, creating contaminations by pairing seemingly incompatible acts, thus educating his audiences.

THE FILLMORE SEMINARS

The educational side of Bill's business was also expressed through the organization of seminars and lectures about the music industry; assiduous Fillmore attendee Paul Sommer tells us about his experience at those seminars:

In the summer of 1969, just after I graduated high school, Bill Graham offered a recording class in San Francisco. The idea was to educate, not train, musicians about the music business. The classes met for two hours [on] Tuesday and Thursday afternoons at Lincoln High School or at Fillmore West (at Market and Van Ness) and every Saturday at one of two different recording studios. His idea was to have his producers, engineers, [and] attorneys along with a local disc jockey educate us on what to expect when and if we performed or went into a recording studio. The entire class was totally free. No charge. The first instructor was David Rubinson, a successful local producer who knew, from experience, what a band could expect when going into a recording studio. Tom Donahue, as one of the most influential disc jockeys in San Francisco, spoke to us about how to get our music on the air; Brian Rohan, Bill's attorney, explained for two hours what musicians needed to do to protect their music; Fred Catero, the chief engineer for Fillmore Records, and Ron Wickersham (later founded Alembic Guitars), an electronics expert who came in from Ampex, explained a lot of the techniques used in a recording studio, from the types of microphones that were used while recording a band to where speakers should be placed. They talked about the setup and the editing of a recording session. Remember this is back in the days of 2" analog recording tape, long before anything digital.

section I   Paul Sommer

FILLMORE SEMINARS

Basic Information

We will met on tuesdays and thursdays for seminars, saturdays for labs. Check your schedule for whichever and whatever.
Sign up to pick a section for the labs on Tuesday July ist.
Lincoln High School requires that there be ABSOLUTELY NO SMOKING on its grounds or in its buildings. They are being gracious, please don't screw it up.
Classes and labs must start on time. Our logistical hangups mean that we only have the exact allotted times indicated on the schedule.
We will start on time so that we can get everything done by the time we have to quit.
The 50¢ lab fee for the Moog seminars is a necessary evil. If you can't make it, don't worry. Anyone who can't pay doesn't have to.

Lincoln High School: Enter only on Quintara at 23rd.
Pacific Recording: Take Bayshore Freeway to Half Moon Bay Freeway, towards Half Moon Bay(Route 92) Get off at El Camino NORTH. One half block on right side, redwood building. Park in the parking lot at the shopping center across the street near lyon's restaurant.

Fillmore Corporation: 1548 Market at Van Ness opposite Fillmore West, on the first floor one flight up.

We have a schedule for meetings up to and including August 7th.
A new schedule will be out when we find another building to replace Lincoln High.
The advanced special seminars will be announced as soon as planned.
Open sessions will be announced as soon as possible.

A notebook is suggested.We will be giving out a lot of printed material

Notes taken by Paul Sommer during the Fillmore seminars in June 1969. *Courtesy of Paul Sommer*

```
                                                        -1-
                        FILLMORE SEMINARS
                        SCHEDULE OF CLASSES
    Session I:          Saturday June 28th     2pm      Fillmore West
                        ORIENTATION AND GENERAL RAP
                        Rubinson, et al

    Session II:         Tuesday July 1st       2pm      Lincoln High School
                        WHAT IS SOUND?
                        Catero
                        A basic discussion of the properties and descriptive
    terms used. Graphic representation.Fundamentals,harmonics,overtones,
    waves,lengths of waves,frequency,pitch,loudness,intensity etc.
                        How do we hear? Objective and subjective.
                        The plucked string: partials, tone chamber,timbre.
                        How the various instruments make their sounds, and
    why they are distinct.
                        RECORDS AS MEDIA
                        Rubinson
                        A general consideration of the record as a medium
    specific media properties. Accesibility as a function of personal
    involvement. Idea to auditor. The solitary auditor. Linear communion
    vs. total comprehension. The record as a cheap piece of plastic.
    Considerations of integrity. The tape or the artists as performer.

                        (note: no meetings July 3rd or 5th--Holiday)
    Session III:        Tuesday July 8th       2pm      Lincoln High School
                        HOW IS SOUND RECORDED?
                        Wickersham,Dangerfield.
                        The basic theory of recording.Microphone as transducer.
    types of microphones,tape recording and disc recording. The theory of
    magnetics.The tape machine; multi-track recording.

    Session IV:         Thursday July 10th     2pm      Lincoln High School
                        AMPLIFICATION
                        Wickersham,Dangerfield
                        The amplification of sound,the establishment of the
    basic paradigm: source--transducer--amplifier--recorder.Units of
    amplification. Basic electronic terminology: watts,ohms,volts,amps.
    Resistance and impedance...Volume Control.
    Session V:          Tuesday July 15th      2pm      Lincoln High School
                        ROYALTY INCOME AND COPYRIGHT LAW
                        Brian Rohan
                        Description of royalties, how they are earned and
    generated. The basic idea of secondary and multiple usage. Basic
    copyright law. Statutory copyright act,mechanical licening and public
    performances. The performing rights societies. Personal appearance
    income and re-use fees. Other media employing multiple usage of
    original performances. Records: The financial and business relationship
    between artists and the companies. The financial responsibilites of
    recording and how the liabilities are shared.
                        How a song is published, how the generated income is
    disbursed. The writer's responsibilities and the publisher's.

    Session VI:         Thursday July 17, Saturday July 19   FILLMORE CORPORATION
    Session VII:        THE ELECTRONIC MUSIC SYNTHESIZER     1548 Market
                        Special lecturer:                    Opposite Fillmore West
                        Pat Gleason

    Five sections :     Section I-2pm to 3:30   Section II-4pm to 5:30 THURSDAY
                        III-1-2:30   IV-3-4:30   V-5-6:30    SATURDAY
                        (Note: there will be a lab fee of 50c FOR THIS ONE
```

Paul also remembers how Bill held meetings explaining the ethics behind his booking strategy for his shows:

In 1969, Bill Graham had Fillmore Records, the Millard (Talent) Agency and Fillmore Management. His two-hour class on live shows turned into a three-and-a-half-hour marathon session at Fillmore West. He had so many stories of performers that he could have continued for many hours more. Bill explained that his concept for most of his shows at the Fillmore was not just to let an audience here the top groups but to educate us too. He would always have three bands play; each band played two sets. There were no assigned seats at the old Fillmore (on Geary Street) or Fillmore West, and everyone could stay the entire night. There were normally a few rows of folding chairs near the front of the stage, and if I got in line early enough, I could get one of those chair seats or sit on the floor in front of the stage and in the front of the chairs. Bill told us that he would book a headliner that could attract the crowd and fill the room, and also would book a local group that needed the exposure like the Sons of Champlin, the Loading Zone, Tower of Power, Cold Blood, Moby Grape, Quicksilver Messenger Service, Blue Cheer, Steve Miller Band, and others. He would also add music from a group that he thought young people should be exposed too, music that he liked: blues, jazz, and R&B. We were all so lucky to be exposed to such great music, up close and affordable.

At the end of our summer seminar, everyone was offered free studio time at one of the studios that Bill Graham and his record label, Fillmore Records, was using at the time. You could be a producer, engineer, or musician. I invited a band I knew, Kidd Afrika, to record a demo that I produced. We were also invited to participate in a real recording session, and I helped on two sessions. One session was when Cold Blood recorded their first album on Fillmore Records. I was there for the recording of "I'm a Good Woman" and "Let Me Down Easy" and was the person that hit the "run" button on the 16-track 2" tape machine when the recording engineer, Fred Catero, said, "Now." The band actually recorded both tunes, one after the other, without stopping. They screwed up the ending, so they did it again. Fred finally spliced the 2"

recording tape and split the one long performance into the two songs that were on the album. The two songs are attached. The other session I helped on was the first Elvin Bishop solo album, shortly after he left the Paul Butterfield Blues Band. I do remember something I had never heard of when Fred Catero recorded some rhythm guitar parts and miced Elvin's Les Paul, just his solid-body guitar, not his amp. Bill Graham and his organization were remarkable for not only providing the opportunity to hear great music in a safe and comfortable environment but also in his generosity to local musicians in an effort to provide valuable knowledge and expertise to anyone and everyone . . . for free.[10]

Session VIII: Tuesday July 22nd   2pm   Lincoln High School
                THE RECORD BUSINESS; The way it is.
                Rubinson
                The practical structure of the record business.
The record from idea to finished master. The internal organizations
of record companies, facets of their operation. Creative vs.business
elements. Independent and corporate record companies. The control
over creative functions. Galvanization of power in the hands of the
creative community. A small talk on how not to get done in.
                DISTRIBUTION AND SALES
A special seminar with some of the leading rack jobbers,one stops,
retailers, company distributors in San Francisco. How a record
gets from the pressing plant to the consumer.

Session IX: Thursday July 24th   2pm.   Lincoln High School
                THE RECORD CONTRACT
                Rubinson and Rohan
                What a record contract is. How it works. The legal
and operative aspects of recording contracts. Presentation of
abstracts from real contracts(anonymous) and explanation of the terms.
The contract as a literal article of faith.
                                Warranties,liabilities,duration,
obligations,percentages,record clubs,options,promotion clauses,foreign
income and royalties, returns,free goods, auditing, stealing, thievery,
and a particularly incisive discussion in the continuing saga of how
not to get done in. The handshake as an obsolete means of communicatio
the verbal agreement as a waste of time. Getting good representation.

Session X: FIRST LABORATORY SESSION

                Saturday July 26th   Pacific Recording Co.
                                                1737 El Camino Real
                In Five sections   San Mateo
                I: 11am-12pm   II:12:30pm-1:30pm   III:2pm-3pm
IV:3:30-4:30   V:5pm-6pm

                Rubinson,Catero, Dangerfield,Wickersham.
                A complete tour and introduction to the recording
studio. Explanation of structures,machines,etc. How the whole thing
works. The five dollar tour. Illustration of the paradigm: source to
recorder. A small discussion about the term professional attitude.

Session XI: Tuesday July 29   2pm   Lincoln High School
                SOUND ALTERATION DEVICES
                Catero,Wickersham,Dangerfield.
                Equalizers,filters,limiters,compressors; the more
complex scheme: source--transducer--amplifier--ALTERATION DEVICES--
volume control--recorder.
                Reverberation: natural and artificial. Straight echo-
live echo chambers,electronic echo chambers,Recreating natural
reverberation characteristics,alteration or exaggeration of natural
reverberation. The different types of artifiacially created reverberati
delay,tape echo devices, round robin reinsertion, surrounding
sound devices. Manipulation of decay. Leslie effects.

Session XII: Thursday July 31st   2pm   Lincoln High School
                RADIO
                Tom Donaghue; special lecturer.
                A group of San Francisco radio professionals will
discuss the different types of formats, the relationship of airplay

to motivating record sales. Private control of public trust. The
obligations of a station to the community. A discussion of the varios
types of radio. Serving all members of the community. Selective
audiences. Demographics of audiences. The commercial radio station
and the publicly owned station.
                Why a station picks a record to play. The difficult
job of selecting playlists. The burden of programming. What a
music director or program director does. How he picks music. What makes
a record get on the air--how to get a record on the air.

Session XIII: Saturday August 2nd   Pacific Recording Co.
              In five sections as before.
              SECOND LABORATORY

              Illustration of basic scheme. Source--transducer--
volume control--recorder. Insertion of alteration devices: eq,filtering,
limiting. A demonstration of equalization--attentuation and boosting.
What effects equalization can have. Use of three tapes and manipulation
of equalization with each tape; special filtering effects. Use of
limiter. Student manipulation of devices.

SessionXIV: Tuesday August 5   2pm   Lincoln High School
                MULTIPLE TRACK RECORDING
                Rubinson,Catero,Dangerfield.
                The theory of multi=track recording. Mono and stereo.
4,8,16,track recording. Recapitulation of loudness as a relative thing.
Balance as the key to relativity. Tracking, sel-syncing,punching in,
how to lay down a track. Listening to the whole, running cues while
tracking. How to make it easy on yourself.
                Mixing. Reduction of multi-track to stereo and
mono. Spatial relationships. Panning, depth of perspectives,special
effects. The concept of mixing as a re-balancing operation, not
therapeutic surgery.Doubling and parallelling, cleaning the track,
keeping the whole in mind,hearing the whole as apposed to tests of
memory.

Session XV: Thursday August 7   2pm   Lincoln High School
                THE PRODUCER
                Rubinson
                The role of the producer. In relation to the
artists, the company,the engineer. Producer as medium, as fascist,
as director. Finding new talent. Development of talent. The advance
as a destructive force. Artist and talent motivation. The producer in
the studio, in the office, in the field. The complete record man.
The necessity or lack thereof for producers. Explaining the artist to
the company, the company to the artist.
                Studio technique. The development of a basic technique
of recording. Application of technique. Choosing the right
technique from the phenomenal repertoire. Tracking vs. live ,
reliance on technical virtuosity, the "honest" recording. Recording
a performance vs. using the tape as the performer. Simplicity as
a tool. Justifying your existence as a destructive motivation.
What a producer must know. Learning to do it by doing it.

When Pete Townshend arrived with the Who in San Francisco on June 16, 1967, and met Bill, he immediately caught the sense of his initiative:

> I think Bill hit on the fact that people *did* want to listen. He certainly created what I came to know as the "electric ballroom syndrome" in America. Which actually changed the face of rock because it made it *listenable* music.[11]

Most of all, Bill had respect for his audience as much as for the musicians, which was the factor that helped the Fillmore gain authority and prestige: Bill profited from the unconditioned receptivity of his audiences to give his musicians room to perform and to let out the essence of their music. It was mainly the English bands that benefited from such a formula: the Who, but also Cream, all hardworking musicians who cut their teeth in the thick, branched-out club circuit in the UK, didn't have to adapt their skills to squeezed thirty-minute sets anymore, but could finally express their full potential without time restrictions and before an audience that was there to listen and to take in whatever the musicians had to offer.

> "We all grew in the electric ballroom," continued Pete; "We grew extraordinarily. We were able to experiment. We were able to take chances. We hadn't done that before because we were more of a pop group. Although we were an R&B band, we were more song-oriented, and we found that we were able to experiment not just on the length of songs but also on song cycles. That led very naturally to quite elaborate and drawn-out sets for us."[12]

Bill's respect for musicians was also expressed through the investment on the best PA system available, which was immediately recognized by Pete and praised at the English press after the Who's return to England. On John Gilliland's microphone, Pete remembered that June 1967 weekend at Bill's venue:

> Those two shows were such a kick in the ass, they really were for us. To go and play at the Fillmore you play to the best possible audience, the nicest people, the most considerate audience, the best possible microphone system, the best possible acoustics—everything is being looked after, and it's always packed for whatever artist, as though as they make sure there's an audience there for everyone.[13]

Fillmore Auditorium, 1805 Geary Boulevard. Friday, June 16, 1967.
Photos taken by Craig Patterson

The impact of the Who at the Fillmore was unprecedented, and the transformation *within* the Who was so radical that Pete was still talking about the effects of playing there even in January 1968, when the band was near the end of a "punitive" tour that took them across Australia and New Zealand; on January 31, he was interviewed at Wellington airport:

> In San Francisco, they somehow combine the best of the English temperament and a listening ability. The atmosphere and the people are very English oriented.[14]

San Francisco also gave Pete a totally new perspective on the nature of live performances, which did not consist of a hasty, predictable showcase of the same repertoire that bands played continually on the rest of the tour but were structured on longer sets on the basis of the audience's receptiveness. The interaction between musician and public influenced one as much as the other:

> In England, audiences differ from town to town radically, and in the States, playing in almost 400 times more different towns with 400 more different kinds of audiences, we're even more at loggerheads as to what to program the audience with. The audience is so precious to us; I mean, we spend incredible amounts of time compiling programs and everything, but eventually once we get out there, we always discard them; we always find that intuition is the best method. It takes intuition and sensitivity, and I mean this is really what makes a live performance a good one.[15]

While the two Fillmore shows on June 16 and 17 introduced the Who to the US underground circuit, the band's first truly important public appearance on American soil occurred on the third day of the Monterey International Pop Festival on Sunday, June 18. The "Love, Flowers & Music" festival, like the stage banter suggested, from embodying the celebration of the blooming Summer of Love, would get to represent the mother of all pop gatherings. It would not just consecrate the Who as a prominent act in the changing music scene, but it would contribute to establishing rock and roll as an art form and the affirmation of the new youth consciousness. As festival producer Lou Adler said in a conversation with the filmmaker who immortalized the event, Donn Alan Pennebaker, the festival aimed to validate rock and roll the same way in which, a decade earlier, Carnegie Hall or the Philharmonic—by hosting jazz acts—helped the genre come out of the underground and clubs circuit and gain wider recognition—recognition as an art form.[16] For Monterey, the Who were among the many musicians who were chosen regardless of the niche they fell into, but for the fact that they were contributing to change the music scene, each in its own way.

FILLMORE, JUNE 16–17, 1967, OFFICIAL LINEUP

Although the original Bill Graham Presents poster for those two nights only report The Who and the Berkeley-based band Loading Zone as only acts, while other sources claim the Loading Zone were replaced last-minute by the yet unknown Santana Blues Band, attendees Craig Patterson and Tom Tallon report that the Loading Zone did play, and the Santana Blues Band was a last-minute, unannounced added act.

San Franciscan Michael Weber remembers that crazy weekend of the Who in California with a singular, both funny and interesting anecdote:

We were young hippies, high and broke, standing outside the Fillmore listening to Bill Graham argue with the Who manager about hauling equipment upstairs. The Who had just got[ten] off the plane and had no equipment people, so we offered to haul equipment for a free ticket to the show. Keep in mind we had never seen the Who and knew little about them. We took another hit and they blew our minds . . . I had never seen anyone destroy their equipment like that. After the show, we were taking equipment downstairs, when they asked if we knew where Monterey was. We said, "Yes, follow us!" We didn't know there was a love festival going on, but anyway, we loaded their equipment in Monterey, got a backstage pass, saw Brian Jones, Jimi, and many more. What a trip—my introduction and weekend with the Who!

Monterey International Pop Festival, Monterey County Fairgrounds, California. Sunday, June 18, 1967. *Photos by Ted Streshinsky. Ted Streshinsky photograph archive, BANC PIC 2004.132—LAN, box 14, file 255, Bancroft Library, University of California, Berkeley*

However iconic the performance of the Who at Monterey was, partly due to D. A. Pennebaker's troupe filming the event, it was not really representative of the band's essence: they were forced into a short twenty-minute set in which they *had* to play out, exasperate, and emphasize their act in order to make their official American debut as effective and convincing as possible within the shortest amount of time. Performance anxiety was diffused backstage before the show and was shared also by Jimi Hendrix, who was, like the Who, under the Track Records label in England and was very aware of Pete's and Keith Moon's antics onstage and didn't want to show himself up. Both the Who and Jimi Hendrix Experience were under pressure, which didn't make either band's performance very spontaneous. "I didn't feel secure at Monterey," remembered Pete, while, on the other hand, he remarked, "I was feeling very secure when we worked for Bill."[17]

While the feedback from Monterey was immediate and on everyone's lips right from the day after, the seed that the more obscure Fillmore performances had sown in the band would work patiently, but far more efficaciously, and would finally lead the Who to express themselves as they really were, which was far more than the shambolic mayhem seen at Monterey, but a band employing power and volume in an extremely sophisticated and articulated way.

Chapter 2

SUMMERTIME BLUES,

JUNE–DECEMBER

1967

America changed the Who and saved them from breaking up; especially San Francisco left a mark that would deeply affect the band's master plan and artistic direction. However, that experience still needed some time to be interiorized, but what's important is that the seed had been sown. The effects would have soon followed.

After the Fillmore in June 1967, the Who found themselves in a crisis, both financial and artistic. On one hand, they were still being affected by noxious contractual obligations dating back to the very early days of the Who, to the Shel Talmy Brunswick/Decca agreement that had been draining the band's finances since the release of their first single, "I Can't Explain," in 1965. At the same time, the smashing of the equipment got more frequent than ever since the band started touring outside the UK. If on one hand it had become something the Who couldn't do without—it had turned into some kind of a brand—it couldn't help but exacerbate the band's financial situation. The Who seemed trapped in an eerie and inevitable repetition compulsion.

On the other hand, the band had to come up with a new album, and Pete, since the release of the *A Quick One / Happy Jack* album, released in late 1966 in the UK and in early 1967 in the US, was admittedly artistically drained. "I got lost," he remembered.[1] What made things even worse was that the Who were doubly committed to write, record, and produce new material and continue to gain recognition in America at the same time by touring. And, just like Frank Zappa would have later taught us in the 1971 Tony Palmer movie *200 Motels*, "Touring can make you crazy!"

In the middle of these conflicts, the Who found themselves crisscrossing America throughout the whole summer of 1967, supporting the Herman's Hermits, recording, and accumulating songs on the days off, between Nashville, Chicago, and Los Angeles, waiting for a definitive album idea that could link all the songs together.

The spark struck Pete's mind on August 15, when he learned about the approval of the Marine Broadcasting Bill, which marked the end for the pirate radio phenomenon in England. To Pete, this event rang as the end of an era that contributed to make bands such as the Who gain their first airings, while the BBC was giving completely different coordinates of the country's music tastes. That is when Pete finally saw the *fil rouge* linking all the new songs together: the new album, which ultimately was titled *The Who Sell Out*, would sound like a continuous pirate radio broadcast in which original songs would be tied together by jingles and advertisements, some of which were even written and played by the band. The album would also represent the zenith of the Who's pop art phase and would consecrate Pete as the true last depositary of the pop tradition. In a wonderful article written by Nik Cohn that appeared in *Eye* magazine in May 1968, the Who of that time, immediately after the release of *The Who Sell Out*, are described as "the last bastion of pop, the final inheritors of a dying tradition." Cohn continues:

> The Who is about the only genuinely pop group still around. Most of the people one considers pop—the Beatles, Beach Boys, Byrds, Donovan, Eric Burdon and so on—aren't really pop at all anymore. Instead, they're ashamed of it, vaguely humiliated by it; it's so trivial, so money conscious. They loathe the whole plastic way of life that originally produced it. Of all those who once accepted pop simply as hard-sell mass entertainment, the Who is virtually the sole survivor. The Who is rock's last great fling, the only group still talking about fast cars and halls and dating, about growing up and timeless teenage hang-ups like pimples, bad breath, making it. About the whole pop thing, in fact. Most of the time, the Who deal in the same things Eddie Cochran was hooked on. Of course, it's not quite as simple as that. Pete Townshend is sharp, analytical, [and] sophisticated and his work relates to Eddie Cochran in roughly the same way that Roy Lichtenstein's Pop Art paintings relate to original comic strips. In other words, he uses the same basic materials but reinterprets them, distances them. "We use very plastic pantomime techniques," he says. "Whereas Cochran's audiences probably took him completely at face value, ours react to us once removed. When we smash up our equipment on stage, for instance, they know that it isn't spontaneous and, oddly enough, they get more excited by it because they know it's a ritual. It's all theatrical—we're acting out their aggressions for them." The Who is best summed up in its last album. At a time when everyone else is churning out hand-me-down surrealism, *The Who Sell Out* is, among things, a return to realism, a bloodbath in advertising and a celebration of everything the rest of the pop world is frantically trying to escape.[2]

As the leadoff song in *The Who Sell Out*, Pete chose "I Can See for Miles." It was written around the same time as "My Generation" and was saved as an ace in the hole in case the band would ever find itself in trouble. What more appropriate time than this? However, like the most emblematic example of heterogony of ends, Pete's ultimate bet that his song could undoubtedly skyrocket into the British Top 10 failed to hit the target: it went no higher than number 9.

The Who were back to square one. Mostly Pete, who, like Nik Cohn wisely observed, "*is* the Who. The future depends almost entirely on Pete. He has the ideas, he writes the songs, he gets everything together."[3] Yet, after the unbelievable blow of "I Can See for Miles," Pete asked himself, "What the hell am I gonna do now?"[4] The pressure was on him, and he had to come up with something, and quick.

Around the same time, caught in this unlucky, bleak dilemma, the Fillmore seed started to show his effects. America, and mostly San Francisco, taught Pete how audiences were expanding their consciousness, and music couldn't be but a reflection of what was happening. Albums were taking over from the pop single, and just like audiences responded so well to extended performances, like happened at the Fillmore, they could surely enjoy longer and more-articulate works. California taught Pete how the audiences' approach to live concerts had gained the shape of a mystical, spiritual searching. They almost gained a transcendent value. It was even more than that: Pete almost saw the live dimension as the *only* real and concrete situation in which music could be made and both artist and the audience could benefit from; after all, even sociologist and philosopher Émile Durkheim described the live concert as one of those situations from which could emerge what he defined "collective effervescence," which is what happens when a community or society comes together and simultaneously communicates the same thought and participates in the same action. As Pete told John Peel in this respect in late 1967, groups such as the Beatles were tending to avoid touring and concentrated only on making albums, automatically making their audiences disappear:

> These groups started off thriving on playing to the public, and now their public seems to have disappeared; they just play to record buyers, and the record buyer audience is nonexistent; it is only existent on the day that they go and buy the record. That's what gives you that audience. Whether or not they listen to it and dig it or understand it is another thing, whereas when you're in a hall you know where your audience is; you can see the expressions on their faces.[5]

Pete finally tuned in with western US audiences' inclinations (without necessarily "turn on" and "drop out," as Timothy Leary encouraged through LSD!). Furthermore, something happened that turned Pete's life upside down, representing the most profound change in his life.

HE IS YOUR LEADER; HE IS YOUR GUIDE:
Discovering Meher Baba

In mid-1967, while in search of direction for himself and for the Who, Pete learned about Meher Baba. It happened through Mike McInnerney, known by many for his artwork for the *Tommy* album, who in 1967 was an artist and illustrator working for the British underground press, doing posters and being art director for the *International Times*. Like he recalled in 1970, "Everybody had opened doors to open houses, like Karen, Pete Townshend's wife. She designed the clothes for my wedding in Hyde Park, and I think it was through her that I first met Pete. And it was just by chance that he was burning for something. . . . I had an immediate strong feeling for Pete and felt that I would like to give him some books on Meher Baba."[6] When Pete read the book that Mike gave him, C. B. Purdom's *The God-Man*, his reaction was so strong that it can only and best be summarized by the words of Rick Chapman, head of Meher Baba Information in Berkeley, who we will get to know better later in the reading:

> No matter what you think about Meher Baba, about Pete or about me: the crucial detail is that in the same way that Haley's comet comes by every seventy-six years, or there's a full eclipse of the sun, the same thing happened to Pete in his becoming aware of Meher Baba, and it influenced everything he did after that, all the songs he wrote: *Tommy*, "Drowned," "The Sea Refuses No River," "Let My Love Open the Door," on and on.[7]

Baba was born Merwan Sheriar Irani on February 25, 1894, in Poona (later spelled Pune), India. The name "Meher

Cow Palace. Saturday, November 18, 1967. *Items courtesy of Sansara-Nirvana Murphy; items photos by Stefano Domenichetti Carlini*

Baba," literally "Compassionate Father," comes from a group of Merwan's early disciples when, in the early 1920s, signs of his spiritual status first started to manifest. He is considered the Avatar of this age—avatar being a Sanskrit word meaning literally "descent of God." Baba defined himself as "the Ancient One," the "Divine Incarnation," and the "God-Man," after which C. B. Purdom named the homonymous book. With the same honesty shown to his disciples—honesty being the path that guards against false modesty and gives the strength of true humility[8]—Baba declared, "When I say I am God, it is not because I have thought about it and concluded that I am God—I know it to be so. Many consider it blasphemy for one to say he is God; but in truth it would be blasphemous for me to say I am not God."[9] Young Merwan became aware of his nature at nineteen, during his second year of college, after he was kissed on the forehead by Hazrat Babajan, one of the five Sadgurus ("Perfect Masters"); like her, also the other four masters (Sai Baba, Upasni Maharaj, Tajuddin Baba, Narayan Maharaj) publicly acknowledged Merwan as the Avatar: "What I am, what I was and what I will be as the Ancient One is always due to the five Perfect Masters of the Age. During the Avataric periods, the five Perfect Masters make God incarnate as man. . . . Babajan, in less than a millionth of a second, made me realize my Ancient State—that I am God—and in the period of seven years, Upasni Maharaj gave me the knowledge that I am the Avatar, the Ancient One."[10] Mystical teachings behind all the great religions indicate that

manifestations of God, or avataric appearances, take place approximately every 700–1,400 years, and Baba is recognized as the manifestation of God on Earth in our era, just like all the other divine personalities throughout the ages—Jesus, Buddha, Rama, Krishna, Zoroaster, and many others—were avatars of their times. Although religions founded upon these avataric appearances of God may differ, and although "God has come again and again in various Forms, has spoken again and again in different words and languages," he has always taught "the same One Truth."[11] Accordingly, although Baba can be understood by every religious tradition, he points out that he doesn't belong to any of them:

> All religions are equal to me. All the castes and creeds are dear to me. But though I appreciate all "isms," religions and political parties for the many good things they seek to achieve, I do not and cannot belong to any of these "isms," religions or political parties, for the Absolute Truth, while equally including them, transcends all of them and leaves no room for separate divisions, which are all equally false. I am not come to establish any cult, society, or organization; nor even to establish a new religion. The religion that I shall give teaches the knowledge of the One behind the many. The book that I shall make people read is the book of the hearts that holds the key to the mystery of life. I shall bring about

a happy blending of the head and the heart. I shall revitalize all religions and cults and bring them together like the beads on one string.[12]

In his life, Baba has never prescribed rituals or practices to his followers, since true spirituality, for him, depends exclusively on how one lives a honest and loving life. To Baba, as Rick Chapman observes, "the avowed atheist who faithfully carries out his work in the world is far more blessed than the man who, claiming to be devoutly religious, shirks his practical everyday responsibilities. 'The greatest sin,' Baba has said, 'is hypocrisy.'"[13]

On July 10, 1925, Baba undertook lifelong silence because of the heavy spiritual work ahead for him, referring to a general increase in chaos and conflict in the world. Also, "because man has been deaf to the principles and precepts laid down by God in the past, in this present Avataric Form I observe Silence."[14] He limited his ways to communicate to the use of an alphabet board and later to a personal language of gestures. This nevertheless did not make his message less authoritative, nor did this change the coordinates of his master plan to "redeem the modern world"; on the contrary, the messages he produced in the most powerful silence were those that reverberated so much to hit and shake the Western world, and Pete Townshend's conscience, like the most outstanding epiphany. As early as 1962, five years before the psychedelic movement would reach its apex of expression with the Summer of Love, Meher Baba's words cut through the idea that mind-altering drugs could be useful in attaining higher states of consciousness. To this day, Baba is one of the decisive causes of the dismantling of the psychedelic movement of the sixties. Although his first statement on the use of drugs dates back to 1962, it was not made public until 1967, and the first event that made the world know about Meher Baba's views on mind-altering substances dates back to the time when Boston College student Bob Dreyfuss discovered this mystic figure, who was said to be the highest spiritual authority of the time, and hitchhiked all the way to India to meet him in November 1965. At that time, Meher Baba was conducting a period of strict isolation with a few disciples in his residence at Meherazad, 9 miles outside the town of Ahmednagar, which would serve as his home for the rest of his life on Earth. When Bob informed Baba of the new and rapidly developing movement in the West that correlated mystical advancement and higher states of consciousness with drug experiences, mainly LSD, which was also known as "reality caps" (short for "capsules"), the Avatar peremptorily and definitely expressed his thoughts on the subject:

No drugs! Many people in India smoke hashish and ganja—they see colors and forms and lights. It makes them elated, but this elation is only temporary; it is a false experience. It gives only an experience of Illusion—it heightens Illusion—and serves as simply another veil over Reality, taking one farther away from it. Tell those who indulge in these drugs (LSD, marijuana and other types) that it is harmful physically, mentally and spiritually.[15]

Smash up!
last photo
October or November 1967

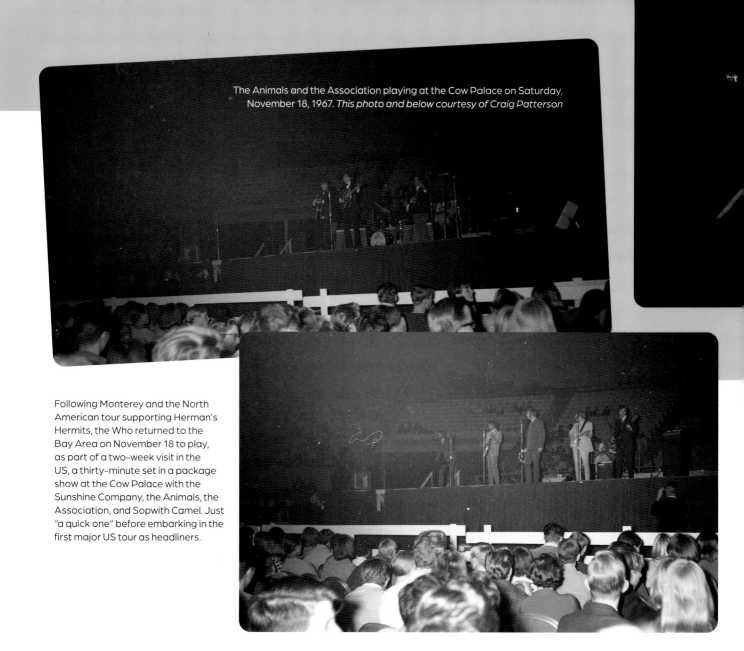

The Animals and the Association playing at the Cow Palace on Saturday, November 18, 1967. *This photo and below courtesy of Craig Patterson*

Following Monterey and the North American tour supporting Herman's Hermits, the Who returned to the Bay Area on November 18 to play, as part of a two-week visit in the US, a thirty-minute set in a package show at the Cow Palace with the Sunshine Company, the Animals, the Association, and Sopwith Camel. Just "a quick one" before embarking in the first major US tour as headliners.

After that, every time young people from the States would visit him, Baba ordered them to go back and dissuade young Americans from taking drugs, acknowledging it as the highest spiritual work to be done in the world today. "The experience which drugs induce are [*sic*] as far removed from reality as is a mirage from water," continued Baba. "No matter how much you pursue the mirage[,] you will never quench your thirst, and the search for Truth through drugs must end in disillusionment."[16]

True to his "Universal Message," in which he explains he has not come to teach, but to awaken, Baba laid down no precepts, and with no legal or moral implications, his message about drugs was aimed to raise awareness on the nature of the psychedelic experience, which was in fact a "delusion within illusion,"[17] and worked only as a distraction from the pursuit of the only event that was worth experiencing; that is,

"God-Realization." This status is achievable only through the natural course of involution of consciousness, through the experience of reality, because once God is attained, it remains a "continual and never-ending experience,"[18] as opposed to drug experiences, which are only temporary.

One might rightly ask whether Baba's message is directed only to spiritual aspirants, or to everyone; in this respect, Baba replied in 1966, "All psychedelic drug use is dangerous and in the long run is harmful, irrespective of whether it is motivated by spiritual aspirations or otherwise." Here, Baba adds an interesting caveat to his statement, remarking that "any drug, when used medically for legitimate diseases under the direct supervision of a medical practitioner, is not impermissible," adding that LSD can be used beneficially for chronic alcoholism, depression, and relief from mental illnesses.[19]

Cow Palace. Saturday, November 18, 1967.
Photos by Sansara-Nirvana Murphy

The Avatar's drug message had such an effect in the psychedelic counterculture that even professor Richard Alpert, who with Timothy Leary had been responsible for spreading the notion of spiritual elevation through psychedelics in the sixties' consciousness, eventually embraced Baba's vision. Leary too acknowledged that "Baba is right," as he told Rick Chapman in 1971,[20] but couldn't leave behind his cliché of LSD advocacy—he was so much into it up to his neck by then—and developed a road show of events named after his era-defining motto "Turn on, tune in, drop out," promising enlightenment through chemical substances.

It wouldn't be long before Pete would find out about Baba's take on drugs, which would draw him even closer to this newly discovered mystic figure and further away from psychedelics, particularly after he had been through, and barely surviving, a recent terrifying trip: while returning from Monterey Pop Festival, on the flight home, Pete tried the infamous "Purple Owsley," a particular kind of acid that had been one of the main attractions at the festival, manufactured by Augustus Owsley Stanley III, Grateful Dead's soundman and first underground chemist to mass-produce LSD. Pete described it as a traumatizing near-death experience.

Chapter 3

SAN FRANCISCO:

FEBRUARY 22, 23, AND 24,

1968

As the new year approached, Pete was finally inspired, focused, and open to whatever would await the Who on the two tours in sight: one across Australia and New Zealand, but mostly, the first major US tour as headliners. The fact that the North American tour started in California, with San Francisco as the second date, appeared as a positive omen.

Pete had carried C. B. Purdom's book through the whole Oceanian tour, as well as a notebook where he jotted down ideas for the Who's next work; the world seemed to synchronically have tuned in with Pete's conscience, since just like Pete found Baba followers in Australia, he did also in California.

Although the Who toured North America by bus, Pete decided to come a few days earlier to California to meet Rick Chapman, head of Meher Baba Information in Berkeley. This was a crucial meeting that would deeply affect Pete and the future of the Who. Rick Chapman himself told me about it:

I knew very little about Pete and the Who at the time that I met him. What I did know is that he was a part of a rock band and that he had become interested in Meher Baba and was in touch with some longtime Baba followers in London. London was a key part of the Advent of the Avatar in this age, inasmuch as England was the first stop of Meher Baba when he left India on his first trip to the West. In that trip, and in the subsequent trips in the 1930s, he attracted the people who would become longtime disciples. Some of those disciples included Kitty Davy; Margaret Craske, who was a ballerina and had a ballet school in London; Delia DeLeon, who was an actress; and others, all of whom lived well beyond Meher Baba's own lifetime and were tremendously influential with those new to Baba, owing to their lifetime of experience with him. All of them served the purpose of being really a relay station for the younger people who came along after Baba passed away or, as it is said about him, "dropped the body"; that's because, for an enlightened being, death doesn't catch you by surprise: you drop your physical body when the time has come. In the case of Pete Townshend and the younger followers of Meher Baba in the London area, Delia DeLeon was the principal contact.

So, when I met Pete, I had literally only seen his name and a photograph of him in a magazine for young people, maybe a year before or some months earlier, and I was alerted by a friend of mine that Pete would be visiting a place in San Francisco that had books available for Meher Baba. At that time, in the 1960s, there were very few sources of literature about Baba, and the only bookstore of that kind in San Francisco was in the office of a group called Sufism Reoriented, which was a Sufi group that had recognized Meher Baba as Avatar and which Baba helped reorient by updating their principles, teaching materials, and their focus.

So, I was told, this guy was going to be over there to visit the book room, and so I went there. I did that because I had been involved in conveying Baba's message to young people for a couple of years by then, so it seemed to make sense to go over and talk to somebody who was in the position of being a rock star communicating with young people and who himself appeared in terms of age to be a peer (Pete, it turns out, is two years younger than I am). So, I went there and simply made his acquaintance while he was looking at books. At one point he said that the band's first gig was in San Jose, and I can't remember how it evolved, but I may have suggested that I drive him down, or he may have said, "What about a lift?" In any case, that afternoon or possibly the next day we drove down from San Francisco, and during the journey I told him about my own meeting with Meher Baba in detail, the one I had had a year and a half earlier. In particular we discussed in great detail Baba's views about drugs, which I was familiar with because, before going to India myself, I had already been in contact with Baba and had been involved in spreading his message about drugs. In that drive down to San Jose, Pete learned that marijuana was included in Baba's prohibited drugs, because Baba was essentially saying that any mind-altering drug used for the purpose of trying to attain a spiritual experience or get high or relax is not useful, and in fact harmful. Interestingly, back then in 1965–66, Baba also said, if taken under the direction of a medical expert, with supervised doses, some of these drugs can be useful in the future in treating certain diseases, such as alcoholism or severe depression. That was fascinating, inasmuch as it is now being studied as a valid potential treatment with such cases. Baba's message and the inclusion of marijuana derivatives in it struck Pete so strongly that he actually stopped using pot at that time. On the spot. That was it.

Later we arrived in San Jose, we got to the hotel, which was a Hilton, and Pete rented a room for me next to his. After some room service and continued talking, we then went to the underground parking area to drive to the concert, which was nearly a disaster, because my silver-gray 1960 Lincoln Continental had a bad solenoid, and after coming down from San Francisco to San Jose, I couldn't start the car! We were in the underground garage of the Hilton Hotel for at least fifteen minutes trying to start it. Pete was more sanguine about it all than I was, probably because he knew that the concert was not going to begin without him. The car finally started, and we drove a short distance, directions courtesy of the front desk.

It was a big deal arriving at the Civic Auditorium, but eventually we drove straight in, as any limousine would do, I parked the car and saw the show, then drove Pete back, this time without the solenoid drama. We went to Pete's modest suite, two basic rooms joined by a mutual door, and relaxed for a while. I had brought a small reel-to-reel tape recorder with me, and I said, "Do you want to tape an interview in which you describe your feelings about what Baba says about drugs?" And Pete said yes. I had never taped an interview, and it was difficult to stay in character as "an interviewer," but nevertheless the result was about twenty to thirty minutes of Pete talking about Baba and drugs. One of the most memorable lines on it was when Pete said, "If Meher Baba says, 'No drugs,' then for me it's law!" Later, over the months and years that followed, I had innumerable occasions to play that tape on San Francisco radio stations that would want to interview me about Meher Baba, as well as elsewhere throughout the country.

After taping that interview, Pete and I went out for a hamburger or some such late-night nosh at about one o'clock in the morning, finding some little deli café nearby, and to my surprise, as I was not at all familiar with how well known Pete was at that time, some kid on the street stopped us and said, "Oh Pete, great to see you! Great show!" and asked for an autograph. Pete complied very thoughtfully, of course, as if that were routine.

That day everything changed for Pete: from that time on, he turned away from using pot. That is not to say that sometime somewhere he did not share someone's joint, but he seriously put an end to his own use generally. In the process of our friendship, however, I introduced him to another bad habit, though: returning from India, I was smoking Indian *beedies*, the Indian peasant cigarettes, four a day inasmuch as Baba had limited more than one of his followers to no more than four cigarettes a day; they cost about a quarter a package at that time for twenty-five of them, and it was either then when we first met or later in our acquaintance that he decided that "if I'm not smoking dope, I've got to do something!" So, he adopted *beedies* as primary smoke, and he occasionally would import dozens of packages, and he would report to me that it was more customs for the *beedies* than the guitar cost!

Back to San Francisco, Pete and I spent a lot of the time the Who was there together. My recollection is that I spent several days with him, repeatedly going over from where I lived in Oakland to a very modest motel, something with "Holiday" in the name but not a Holiday Inn or the Holiday Lodge that Meher Baba had stayed in; it was a different motel on Van Ness Avenue, and it was quite a humble place, an ordinary motel, just about a mile down the road from where the Sufi center was located. I would take most meals with him and the band; all of them were quite ordinary at the time. If you have the information as to how long Pete was in San Francisco, that would tell you how many days I stayed there. I would drive over there every day, and one day he also came back over with me to Oakland, visiting the place I was staying and the office of Meher Baba Information, which was in the house where I was staying in the Oakland hills. I think it was on a later trip that he actually stayed over one night in that house. Pete and I came to be really good friends.[1]

Fillmore Auditorium, Thursday, February 22, 1968: Leslie West in a feather cape playing in The Vagrants, opening act for the Who. He plays through an 8 × 10 Marshall model 2034 cabinet stacked on top of two Marshall 4 × 12 cabinets. See also a rare photo of Keith Emerson attacking his Hammond organ, playing in the last-minute added act The Nice. Photos of the Who are from the first set. *Photos by Paul Sommer*

While the first show of the new US tour, on February 21 in San Jose, was a very good one, but not particularly different from the Who's general standard of that time, the band saved their highlights for the three days ahead of them: the next day after the San Jose show, like Rick Chapman anticipated, the Who made their triumphant return in San Francisco, where they would play for three nights.

One of the many aspects that made those shows very special was the other acts that Bill Graham had chosen to pair the Who with: first of all, there was none other than Cannonball Adderley. He was playing with his brother Nat on cornet, Victor Gaskin on double bass, Roy McCurdy on drums, and Joe Zawinul on piano (see page 147), and his "Tengo Tango" was one of those tracks that deeply affected Pete as a young player. Pete was, to say the least, enthusiastic and honored to share the bill with these jazz musicians and was even more so for receiving positive feedback from them after the Who's performances: "It was interesting to feel that what we were doing was acceptable to people like that."[2] The presence of the Cannonball Adderley Quintet brought the lysergic Fillmore scene back a decade, to the days of the San Francisco jazz era of the 1950s, in which Cannonball and his brother Nat had given their contribution and left their mark with the live album *The Cannonball Adderley Quintet in San Francisco* (Riverside, 1959).

To round out the unique bill, there was the English band the Nice, a last-minute unannounced act featuring Keith Emerson on Hammond organ, and the Vagrants, featuring what would become Mountain guitarist and good friend of the Who, Leslie West.

For all three nights, February 22 at the Fillmore and 23–24 at Winterland, from 7:00 p.m. to 2:00 a.m., the four bands followed each other in this sequence: the opening act were the Vagrants, who played a forty-five-minute set, then Cannonball Adderley, also for forty-five minutes; the unannounced middle act, the Nice, did a single sixty-minute set, which was followed by the first Who set, which lasted forty-five minutes. Then the lineup repeated with the second forty-five-minute set by the Vagrants, a longer set for middle act Cannonball Adderley, and finally the Who as closing act. The same audience stayed all night and witnessed two forty-five-minute sets of completely different music by the Who.

FILLMORE AUDITORIUM:
Thursday, February 22, 1968

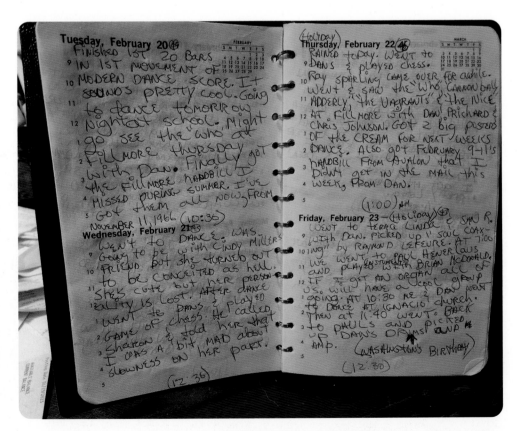

Four days in the life of a Who fan: Douglas P. Bratt's diary entries from February 1968 about getting tickets and attending the Who concert at the Fillmore on February 22. *Courtesy of Douglas P. Bratt*

SAN FRANCISCO: FEBRUARY 22, 23, AND 24, 1968

Fillmore Auditorium, Thursday, February 22, 1968: The Vagrants opening for the Who. Attendee Paul Sommer recalls: "I heard Bill Graham chewing out the band at the beginning of their second set, 'You have the same people here as your first set' ... because they were repeating their first set. I think Leslie West said, 'We don't know any more tunes!'" *Photos by Paul Sommer*

The Fillmore hummed with anticipation for the return of the Who in town. It is reported by attendee Michael E. Tassone that local band Blue Cheer was also in the audience. They also were on the bill the night before in San Jose, making an interesting pair with the Who, since both bands had the song "Summertime Blues" in their set lists. However, while the Who had made Eddie Cochran's classic a live favorite, having played it onstage for over a year, they still hadn't recorded it, unlike Blue Cheer, who made it the hit single off their debut album *Vincebus Eruptum*, which had just been released. Although Blue Cheer's debut work was greeted as "the loudest record ever made,"[3] the Who made sure to remind everyone they were the loudest act *live*: at the Fillmore, on February 22, when the Who ripped into their version of "Summertime Blues," it was fun for the audience to watch Blue Cheer standing in front of the room with their mouths gape open as they were overwhelmed by the Who's version.[4]

Nineteen-year-old Steven Novak happened to be in the Vagrants' party and gives his recollections from being backstage at the Fillmore on February 22:

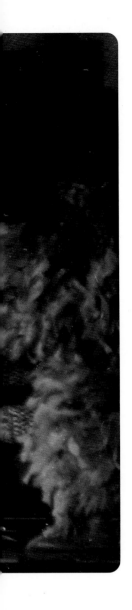

Fillmore Auditorium dressing room. A drowsy Pete dresses up for the first set. *Photographs by Frank Zinn (courtesy of Richard Martin Frost)*

The Vagrants were a very big New York City band that played all over New York and Long Island, and they could have been the biggest group to come out of New York, but that became the Young Rascals. The Vagrants released a song called "Respect," on ATCO, and one week later, Aretha Franklin released it and blew it out of the water. The matter of that week ended their trip to stardom, but if you lived in New York between 1965 and 1969, the Vagrants were gigantic. I used to see them every weekend in a club on Long Island called the Action House.

I was with them when they played in San Francisco with the Who, Cannonball Adderley, and the Nice. I didn't go with them; I went with a friend who was a travel agent, and we happened to hang out with the Vagrants.

Fillmore Auditorium dressing room before the Who's first set, February 22, 1968. Pianist Joe Zawinul, from the Cannonball Adderley Quintet, sits behind Roger, who is studying the set list. *Photograph by Frank Zinn (courtesy of Richard Martin Frost)*

I said to my father, "I'm going to California." "No, you're not," he said, but I picked up and went anyway. I must have been nineteen, and that was my first introduction to psychedelics and the San Francisco music scene: I remember being in the Fillmore dressing room, and Augustus Owsley III was there and was giving out his Orange Sunshine LSD; the Who had all their beer in the dressing room, and we drank it all! We didn't figure it was big deal, but it was their beer, so whatever time they went for sound check and realized we drank all their beer made Pete and Roger very upset! I can remember distinctly one moment in which Roger Daltrey asked Peter Townshend, "Have you seen me hat?," and Pete said, "Your 'at is on your 'ead!"[5]

For the return of the Who at the Fillmore, John Entwistle, who was in charge of the set lists at that time,[6] came up with a very special selection of "hits & misses" that left the auditorium's public dumbstruck. That night, the Who treated the San Francisco audience with a seven-minute-long version of "Run Run Run," including a rare drum solo by Keith. When years later Moonie admitted to disliking solos, someone should have reminded him about this Fillmore show! After a very groovy version of "I Can't Explain," slayed by Pete on his red Gibson ES-335, the Who dusted off a very rare "Don't Look Away," introduced by John, before then crashing into "Boris the Spider" [and] "Easy Goin' Guy," introduced by the Ox as "My Way," a very long version of the mini opera "A Quick One, While He's Away," and then "I Can See for Miles," which Pete, a little bittersweetly, introduced as

our last record, which we don't play on the stage, 'cept here. The reason we don't play it onstage is because . . . outside of here we played it in England mostly and Australia. . . . And it wasn't a hit in England for real; it was kind of a hit, but it wasn't the kind of hit it was here.[7]

Fillmore Auditorium dressing room, before the first set. Fashion note: during the first set, Pete wore his usual white frilly shirt of the time under his Pearly King golden jacket, while he wore a blue T-shirt under it during the second set. *Photographs by Frank Zinn (courtesy of Richard Martin Frost)*

Had it not been for Steve Cowley, who brought a reel-to-reel tape recorder with him that night, we wouldn't have had any evidence of what the Who played at their return to the Fillmore, and it would have fallen silent and abandoned to "the foggy ruins of time," in Bob Dylan's words.

Steve had enough tape to bring us proof of the only existing live version of "I Can See for Miles" to be captured around its release, but unfortunately, not enough tape to capture it in its entirety. Just before the first refrain, the recording stops abruptly, but glorious opening chords of what sounds like an incredibly inspired version of "Substitute" crash in—the Who had just gotten their baptism of fire at Bill Graham's other venue: Winterland.

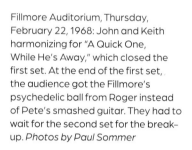

Fillmore Auditorium, Thursday, February 22, 1968: John and Keith harmonizing for "A Quick One, While He's Away," which closed the first set. At the end of the first set, the audience got the Fillmore's psychedelic ball from Roger instead of Pete's smashed guitar. They had to wait for the second set for the break-up. *Photos by Paul Sommer*

Fillmore Auditorium. Thursday, February 22, 1968 (second set). © *Jim Marshall Photography LLC*

WINTERLAND

Winterland. Post and Steiner Streets. *Photo by Shigeto Murase*

Born as New Dreamland Auditorium in 1928, Winterland served as an ice-skating rink that often hosted Eddie and Roy Shipstad's touring show of the "Ice Follies," but also boxing matches and opera in the '50s, before Bill Graham brought over his productions, starting on September 23, 1966, with six nights with Jefferson Airplane, Butterfield Blues Band, and Muddy Waters. Many members of the youth community that entered Winterland for the first time as kids in the 1950s, accompanied by their parents to see basketball games or funny characters on skates, found a different atmosphere at their return to the building ten years later—an atmosphere far from the innocence of childhood. A second venue that could complement Bill's shows became a necessity, since attendance was growing exponentially at the Fillmore, which had a maximum legal capacity of nine hundred. With its 5,400 capacity, the nearby Winterland, located on Post and Steiner Streets, literally two blocks away from the Fillmore, became a venue that could host wider audiences on Fridays and Saturdays, while the Fillmore ended up working for Thursdays

and sometimes Sundays. At Winterland, the doors opened at 7:00 p.m. and the bands followed each other, on a simple, rectangular open stage. There were no curtains: the audience witnessed everything that would be going on before, between, and after sets.

When in 1971 Bill decided to close Fillmore West (after having moved the scene in July 1968 from the original Fillmore to this other venue, formerly the Carousel Ballroom, on 10 South Van Ness), from its complementary function Winterland became Bill's main venue and presented acts on a regular basis. It became the quintessential rock arena of the '70s where legendary events took place. To name a few, the Rolling Stones' comeback in San Francisco in June 1972, after two and a half years of absence following the Altamont disaster on December 6, 1969; the recording of Peter Frampton's *Frampton Comes Alive!* album; and the farewell concert of the Band on Thanksgiving Day 1976, let alone all New Year's Eves from 1967 until the venue's closing on December 31, 1978 . . . also, the comeback of the Who in San Francisco on March 27 and 28, 1976, as a makeup pair of appearances since the infamous Cow Palace concert on November 20, 1973, in which Keith Moon passed out multiple times due to the ingestion of elephant tranquilizers. That's, of course, another story, and while we'll get to the 1976 concerts later, back to February 1968: at their first time at Winterland, the Who found a very different setting than they would find in the seventies.

In addition to the audience, the wide concert hall also was different then: in the sixties, the stage was positioned on the south side of the hall, the long side. It was still standing room only, and the balcony seats were unused and so would remain until the seventies, when the stage would be brought to one of the narrower sides of the venue. Also, gone would be the large panels and screens that, in the sixties, Bill, together with his partner Jim Haynie, carried every Thursday night, after each Fillmore concert, across Geary Boulevard and into Winterland, and onto which Glenn McKay's "Headlights" and Ray Andersen's "Holy See" immersive light shows accompanied the Friday and Saturday performances. Psychedelia would make way for lasers pyrotechnics, but in those early 1968 nights, the Who were still one with the light shows.

Winterland may not be as iconic as the Fillmore, and it definitely was not a ballroom, or a place specifically designed for music; still, despite that, and maybe because of it being an unusual setting for live music, it holds a special place in many people's hearts and memories. Mark d'Ercole looks back to "that old building" with nostalgia and great affection:

> I miss Winterland . . . It was a magical place, it really was. It was so unusual seeing a show there because the place was so different from any other place you could go to. The upper deck had 5–6 rows of seats, so you were sitting about 40 feet away, up in the air, and could see the whole stage, with the light show going right in front of you. The entire back wall had a big sheet that they showed the light show on. The old Fillmore was pretty barebones, it was just this room, it wasn't very big, with an overwhelming volume. Fillmore West had an outer area that had couches in it, so you could either sit on the couches, or sit on the floor (they had rugs everywhere), and the sound was perfect in that place. Winterland was more about the atmosphere of the place—the people. The shows there were so special. I think it was the shape of the place, it acted like a concave thing that would bring the music back at you.

BEFORE LIVE AT THE FILLMORE EAST 1968 . . . "LIVE IN SAN FRANCISCO"?

Sources report that the three nights in San Francisco, February 22, 23, and 24, saw the band attempting a live recording, supervised by Kit Lambert and engineered by Bill Halverson, two months before the famous Fillmore East shows of April 5 and 6.[8]

It would have made sense: What better occasion than recording the Who in San Francisco? However, after thorough archival research through photographic archives documenting all three nights, one at the Fillmore and two at Winterland, no visual proof of any professional recording equipment has surfaced, except one: on a particular shot taken by the late Douglas Kent Hall, part of a large collection of photos preserved at Princeton University Library, all from Winterland on February 23, a microphone can be seen placed on top of Keith's drum kit (see pages 118 and 122). This would suggest that a possible soundboard recording could have been attempted on Friday, February 23, but still nothing official has emerged from the band's vault. Furthermore, although it is believed that such a recording was engineered by Bill Halverson, Bill denies having been involved in this operation and clearly stated that he was not in San Francisco with the Who.[9]

So far, the only audible proof from that night is represented, again, by Steve Cowley's tape.

SAN FRANCISCO: FEBRUARY 22, 23, AND 24, 1968

Not only did the first Winterland show reportedly anticipate a recording attempt that the Who would approach more rigorously a couple of months later at Fillmore East in New York, it also anticipated an episode that the following year, 1969, would occur on a bigger stage, before a definitely wider audience—Woodstock. The "Peace, Love & Music" themes that accompanied the name of the legendary festival and were meant to set it in the right vibes were nevertheless suspended during the Who's set in the early Sunday morning, when Yippie leader Abbie Hoffman unexpectedly came onstage, approached Pete's microphone, and tried to wake up the tired audience's conscience regarding MC5's manager John Sinclair being arrested for the possession of two joints. Bad luck for Abbie that the Who happened to be halfway through one of the first major US performances of their brand-new, groundbreaking album *Tommy*, and nothing in that particular moment was more important for Pete than revealing the parabola of the senses-deprived boy to the Who's first major audience. Even though Pete sympathized with Abbie Hoffman, as he later admitted,[10] that uncalled-for speech made Abbie gain Pete's guitar bumped on his head, making it one of the absolute highlights of the festival.

The Woodstock festival was attended by young people coming from all over the US, and there surely must have been some from California who, a year earlier, had already seen the Who play at Winterland. For these attendees, Abbie Hoffman's incident must have felt like déjà vu, since something similar occurred at Bill Graham's concert hall. As can be heard from Steve Cowley's tape from Winterland, stage banters between songs are continually disturbed by a guy who keeps provoking Pete, daring him to smash his guitar on his hands: "He's trying to provoke me to smash him up with me guitar!" Pete tells the crowd.[11] Apparently, as Richard Martin Frost, friend of the late photographer Frank Zinn, reports, the guy started it all by initially trying to grab Roger by the ankles. This apparently irritated Pete, who challenged the guy. The guy then started playing "chicken" with Pete by putting his hand on the stage, daring Pete.[12] They went back and forth a few times until the inevitable happened: the teases, continued throughout the set, as can be heard from Steve's recording, are initially ignored by Pete, but they finally become a drag to the point that the guy gets his wish, which is Pete's Fender smashed on his hands. The audience cheers with applause, and Pete justifies the gesture, saying to the microphone, "It's exactly what you wanted; it's exactly what you wanted." The episode was so shocking that photographer Frank Zinn named the strip of negatives immortalizing that moment "Townshend Terror at Winterland" (see pages 111 and 112).

What we can't hear of this episode from Steve Cowley's recording, we can see from rare shots taken by the late Douglas Kent Hall (see pages 107 and 108 for images of the guy in the crowd annoying Pete and Roger) and read about in the memories of some who were there, such as James Terry Leary, Michael Lazarus Scott, and the late guitarist of the band Savage Resurrection, JP Palmer.

James Terry Leary:

Who??

The time I grew up in the late 1960s and early 1970s San Francisco Bay Area was a music lover's dream.

A fellow named Bill Graham began putting on shows featuring a plethora of young, local musicians who were forming bands playing original rock-and-roll music that had its roots in folk music and the early "beat" movement of coffee shops, poetry, and bongo drums.

A very cool and creative scene for young, hungry artists striving to be seen and heard. All of this in itself was a recipe for something special, but the introduction of an unexpected ingredient morphed it into a phenomenon.

That ingredient was LSD.

Suddenly San Francisco was the place to be, the hub of a new way of dressing, growing your hair . . . and playing a new style of rock-and-roll music.

Bill Graham opened the Fillmore Auditorium and began promoting the new bands, pairing them in shows with awesome established jazz musicians who had been coming to the city for years, playing in small clubs like the Purple Onion, Jimbo's Bop City, the Jazz Workshop, and Keystone Korner . . . and the new, young bands from the British Invasion like the Kinks, the Yardbirds, the Rolling Stones . . . and the Who.

Can you imagine paying $2.00 and seeing Miles Davis, Janis Joplin, and the Yardbirds?

Shows like that were happening every night during this mythical never-to-be-repeated time in history, and you just never knew what these new bands were going to do to express their art, [to] stand out in this new environment.

Blow your mind . . . like the Who.

The first time I saw the Who was at the Fillmore in June of 1967. I honestly can't remember what band or bands played with them . . . because they blew my mind.

They came out all dressed differently but similarly in satin Edwardian coats with frilly shirts and beautiful boots, looking like some kind of English royalty about to dance a gavotte or a minuet . . . until they started playing.

Then they were suddenly an explosion of sound and movement that was impossible to take in all at once: Pete Townshend windmilling his arms, leaping in the air, and sliding across the stage on his knees; Roger Daltrey dancing as he sang and whipping his microphone with a 30-foot cord out over the heads of the audience between vocal lines and bringing it back into his hands, timed perfectly to sing the next line; Keith Moon, a tiny, impossible cacophony of perfection, pounding out the beats of their tunes and firing drumsticks into the audience and picking up new ones without missing a beat . . . and John Entwistle, standing stalwart still as if he was the anchor that kept the whole band from just flying off the stage like a tornado.

They finished their set by destroying their instruments and blowing up Moon's drums with some sort of device that created a cloud of smoke that they used to disappear like magicians . . .

The whole thing had the strange effect of leaving everyone in the room physically exhausted. It was rude and violent and loud and in your face . . . and unforgettable and beautiful . . . what a strange combination!

The next time I saw them was nearly a year later in February of 1968 at a larger venue, Winterland. The opening act was an East Coast band called the Vagrants. They featured a 3-plus-sized lead guitarist named Leslie West. Leslie was later to become pretty famous in a band called Mountain.

He played a screaming lead guitar on a Gibson Les Paul Junior that looked like a ukulele on him. . . . The Vagrants were good, but they were in the impossible position of keeping a crowd that was ready for the energy and violent intent of the Who entertained. . . . The crowd was screaming for the Who the entire time the Vagrants were onstage, but finally cheered with pleasure when they announced

their last tune. . . . So, the Vagrants are plugging away at their finale when, [in] what I guess was a misguided attempt to upstage the Who, they set off an explosive device that created a smoke cloud that they disappeared behind.

The problem was that the device was in a metal electrical box that was sent flying into the crowd and hit a young woman in the face. . . . She was taken away by medical staff. I heard later that she was okay.

Bill Graham came onstage and made a big deal of saying that the Vagrants were assholes and would never play one of his venues again.

The Who came out, did their typically amazing set . . . and blew up the stage as usual at the end of "My Generation."

Gotta love those guys![13]

James Terry Leary spotted himself in one of the photos from Winterland, on February 23, featured in this book (see bottom photo on page 107 and middle photo on page 108): he's the long-haired guy in front of the stage. "I remember having my chin on the stage at a couple of points; it was something I loved doing back then. The Fillmore stage was the same way," Terry told me.

Michael Lazarus Scott:

An exchange student from England turned me on to the Who's second album, *Happy Jack*. I bought it, loved it, and couldn't wait to see the Who live. Before that was to happen, their third album, *The Who Sell Out*, was released, and it is still one of my favorites. On the same day as this concert, my favorite San Francisco band, Quicksilver Messenger Service, was playing at the Straight Theater on Haight Street. My friends had decided to go see them, and as I rarely missed an opportunity to see them, I was left with a difficult choice. I opted for the Who and hitchhiked from Berkeley to the venue. I'm sure my best friend, Michael Lindberg, would have gone with me, but he was in Vietnam fighting that shitty war, so I went by myself. The Who came on with total flash! Pete windmilling his Fender, wearing a gold-spangled coat and ruffled shirt. Moon the Loon all over his circus-painted double kit, mugging it up and going from perfect cadence, twirling, throwing, and catching his sticks, into complete utter chaos and back again. The most astounding and entertaining drummer I have ever seen. The Ox stalwart like a rock, playing lead bass in his black suit. Roger was before his masculine, curly-haired Tommy look. Tonight, he was resplendent with piled-high bouffant curls and what looked like a gold matador outfit. As the fabulous rock-and-roll and dramatic performance unfurled, there appeared to be a fellow right up front who seemed not too enthused with it all. He had shoulder-length blonde hair and was wearing a letterman's jacket, looking like a jock who had grown out his hair. Back in these days the audience sat on the floor, many too loaded to stand. The letterman, apparently having an issue with Roger's appearance, kept standing up, gesturing to Rog and exhorting the crowd. What he was saying I could not hear, but it was obviously derogatory and of a venomous nature. To Roger's credit, he ignored the imbecile. Pete, however, was not so inclined. After finishing the number, he stepped to the mic and said, "I wish the bloke up front would quit hassling me lead singer!" During the next song the jock starts back up worse than before. Pete, stage right, suddenly whips off his guitar, brandishing it by the neck like an axe, and careens across the stage and savagely swings it at the jock's head. The twit sees him and at the last millisecond turns, the guitar just missing his noggin. He runs through the crowd, who have all jumped to their feet and are going wild. Throughout it all, the rock has never stopped. Pete puts his axe back on and just loses it completely, jumping up and down, windmilling, playing as if there will be no tomorrow. It is truly glorious! The most rock-and-roll thing I have ever witnessed! When the song finally climaxes, a flustered, out-of-breath Pete attempts to quiet us and says something to the effect of "I don't condone violence, but I won't put up with no shit either!" The four times I've seen the "'Orrible Who," this was the only performance that they destroyed their instruments during the finale. Moon kicked over his whole kit. Roger had his mic feeding back into the amps. Pete runs his axe in and out of the speakers before finally throwing it high into the air as he walks off. The guitar hits the stage with a final death gasp. It was deafening loud with smoke everywhere, looking like a war had been fought. Utter carnage! I have perused many books on the Who and have never found mention

of this incident. As I was there alone, I've never had anyone to substantiate my story. Last week I made reference to JP Palmer, then the lead guitarist with the Savage Resurrection, who said he was at this concert and remembered it as such. It is good to have some credence to it all. This concert made me a Who fan for life![14]

JP Palmer:

My name is JP Palmer, and I am originally from the San Francisco Bay Area. I played in a few groups in the mid to late '60s, and the Who were one of my favorite British groups. The bands that I played with at the time all knew several of the Who's songs and would get excited whenever they would come to the Bay Area to perform. I saw them, in total, five times live.

Some of the most interesting and more memorable concerts were at the old, original Fillmore Auditorium, which most groups from England played at. It cost about $3 to get in, I believe. Many times, the entire group (our band) would go and see the concerts. It was at one of these concerts that some crazy things happened onstage and off (backstage).

At Winterland, on February 23, 1968, the Who were performing "I Can't Explain" and were about halfway through the song, when somewhat of a disturbance was taking place between a guy who was leaning on the stage, taunting Roger, and yelling at Pete. I was about 8 feet away, closer to Pete's side of the stage, when Pete looked quite upset, so he slung his guitar off his shoulder and slammed the butt of it down on the guy's hands. You could hear the guy scream even with the music playing. Security was right there and hauled the guy off. The Who continued to play.

Another memorable concert, the first time of the Who at the Fillmore in June 1967, the drummer and I got led to the backstage room where the band was relaxing. Roger had been out around the corner to a small liquor store and came into the backstage area and was handing out packages of Winston cigarettes, of which he tossed a pack at me. Roger was in a joyful mood. There were a few girls and guys mulling about talking to each of the Who. Pete was sitting very stoic looking, nursing a deep gouge in his right hand which happened during their set. John sat quietly in a chair talking to a girl. When, all of a sudden, we heard a loud jungle, Tarzan type of scream, and it was coming from the top of a short staircase. Out jumped Keith wearing white boxers with big red hearts on them and proceeded to dive headfirst into a large garbage can below. Everyone screamed with laughter. I could not believe what I saw. Amazing. These are just a few of my memories of that time. I did see and meet Hendrix, Cream, and several others at the old Fillmore . . . great times![15]

Other than serving as proof for the identification of the guy annoying Pete and Roger, Douglas Kent Hall's photos also reveal the presence of a mysterious kid sitting on John's side of the stage (see pages 101, 103, 106 to 111, and 123); this might be Dennis McCoy, who also photographed the show and whose shots and great story from that night appear on Joe Giorgianni's Who page (https://www.thewho.org/tales/dennis.htm).

From the little that can be heard, and from much of what has been told by the fortunate ones who were there on those Friday and Saturday nights at Winterland, the Who embodied the quintessence of the rock-and-roll ethos: caught in the middle of a visible transformation, divided between the pop icons that used to be and the band that they were becoming, the Who were bringing out an essence that could not be found anywhere, not even in their latest release, *The Who Sell Out*, but right there onstage, *live*. The Who embodied the rock-and-roll essence and glorified their frustrations, playing and singing their hearts and guts out, as if there was no tomorrow.

Photograph by Frank Zinn (courtesy of Richard Martin Frost).

WINTERLAND: FRIDAY, FEBRUARY 23, 1968

A STORY IN PHOTOS

SET LIST*

IRST SET:

SUBSTITUTE"

PICTURES OF LILY"

SUMMERTIME BLUES"

TATTOO"

'M A BOY"

HAPPY JACK"

RELAX"

MY WAY (EASY GOIN' GUY)"

CAN SEE FOR MILES"

SECOND SET:

"RUN RUN RUN"

"I CAN'T EXPLAIN"

"DON'T LOOK AWAY"

"BORIS THE SPIDER"

"A QUICK ONE, WHILE HE'S AWAY"

"SHAKIN' ALL OVER"

"MY GENERATION"

*A part from the songs "Substitute" and "Pictures of Lily" and the introductions to "Tattoo" and "I'm a Boy," which were recorded by Steve Cowley, the rest of the set list is a hypothetical reconstruction of what the Who might have played on the first Winterland night. The song selection and sequence are derived from the observation of set lists from the previous two nights in San Jose and at the Fillmore (twenty minutes of which were recorded by Steve Cowley), and a careful analysis of photos by Douglas Kent Hall and Frank Zinn from February 23, from which can be deduced that Pete closed the first set playing a rare Coral Hornet guitar (see page 113), which could have been used for the equally rare "I Can See for Miles"; "A Quick One, While He's Away" must have been played in the second set, like the photo of John and Keith harmonizing together from the second set indicates.

John and Keith in San Francisco on Friday, February 23, before their first Winterland appearance. A couple of the photos Douglas Kent Hall took on that day were used for Sunn equipment advertisements. *Courtesy of Dawn Hall Estate of Douglas Kent Hall; scans from original negatives preserved at Princeton University Library*

BUCK MUNGER AND
THE LOST INTERVIEW
by Steve Caraway

Courtesy of Dawn Hall Estate of Douglas Kent Hall;
scans from original negatives preserved
at Princeton University Library

In these two shots, John is depicted with Buck Munger, who at the time was national promotion director for Sunn amplifiers, which the Who were using and endorsing in their 1968 North American tour. Buck Munger crossed paths with the Who for the first time the year before at the Monterey Pop Festival; there, Buck had to meet the band for a meeting after John Entwistle got an interest in Sunn equipment, having borrowed a 200S unit from the Moody Blues earlier on. The Who had also learned about Sunn equipment from seeing the Rolling Stones perform on *Hullabaloo* with the Kingsmen, whose groundbreaking hit "Louie Louie" helped the amplifying company gain recognition. The connection with Munger brought the Who to start endorsing Sunn in their summer 1967 North American tour with the Herman's Hermits. This connection brought Buck Munger close to the Who, contributing to a fond friendship especially with John. In a rare tape from 1976 I discovered in 2020, John Entwistle tells *Guitar Player* magazine journalist and photographer Steve Caraway about Buck Munger, describing him as drinking partner and friend. Buck would remain close to

John until the bass player's last day, on June 9, 2002. In another rare tape I discovered, a very detailed and in-depth interview of Steve Caraway with Buck Munger is featured, in which exclusive information and details about the Who's relationship with Sunn are revealed. This interview was made on the phone from Steve Caraway's apartment and recorded by him on cassette sometime before the Who's appearance at "Days on the Green" October 1976 concerts:

♪ **STEVE CARAWAY:** Explain to me briefly your first association with the Who and some of the equipment specs and their needs.

♪ **BUCK MUNGER:** I first met the Who when they were, I think, in their first or second American tour; I think it was the beginning of their second, and they had been on the road with the Blues Magoos, who used Sunn bass amplifiers, and they found those to be the most powerful and largest that they had seen in this country. They were very much into, relatively speaker-configuration-wise, the same thing they're into now, 4 × 12 cabinets and things like that, and they were really looking for a relationship with a company who could eventually come to produce the units that they already knew they needed, rather than being convinced to use any specific piece of equipment that we already made. So, this is probably late '67.

♪ **S.C.:** Were they looking at the Sunn tubes stuff, right?

♪ **B.M.:** I think John Entwistle was naturally the first to be turned on to the Sunn equipment because he was the bass player, and the first unit Sunn signed was Norm Sundholm, who was the bass player in the Kingsmen, and our big leader in the market was the 200S 65W RMS tube top. So, based on their contact with the units with the Blues Magoos, they tried to get in touch with us to get them set up for the second American tour, and at the same time that this was happening, which is really funny, they were doing their first television

shows and Vox had gotten to them to use (Vox had a thing with a television show and provided equipment for them), and then after Vox provided that equipment for them, they took the receipt for receiving the equipment for the show—to mean an endorsement—and they published in Billboard a little blurb saying, "The Who endorse Vox equipments," so even though they had contacted me, I was stirring this Vox endorsement in their face and I asked them to clarify that [laughs], and they did; they wrote me a nice letter saying, "We have never endorsed Vox equipment," and they explained to me that it was for the use on that television show. So, we fixed them up for that next tour. The relationship was very out front as far as the destruction of the equipment; in other words, the Sunn management was not aware that their trip was destroying equipment, but I became aware of that very soon, but I also became aware that wherever they played, such attention was drawn to the equipment because of that. Pete Townshend was the man in fact who was doing the negotiation for the band in those days, and, with relatively little help, their management, Kit Lambert and Chris Stamp, were primarily concerned with the marketing of their records and really didn't, to my knowledge, participate in the touring aspect quite as much. Pete made those decisions, and he handled the equipment and so on. In the negotiation, he was very out front with me as regards the destruction of the equipment. We were discussing about a fourteen-page, five-year, ironclad, very conservative American legal document, and Peter was aware that this was a very heavy commitment on his part, because he was firstly aware that we would have no agreement as long as there was even a possibility that they had signed an agreement with another company, but the thing that impressed me the most about this was how out front was he about the fact that that would in fact possibly and probably take place, but they would be responsible for refurbishing the equipment, and this is where Bob Pridden came in. Pridden really had to keep that stuff going on the run. Most of the time that Peter would attack the equipment, he would rim a speaker, and all Bob would have to do is pop out the speaker and put in another one. One thing here that's really important, to my knowledge, and I don't know that this is absolutely correct, but all the time that I worked with them, they never carried any phony equipment to break up. Everything they broke up was real and functioning on-the-stage stuff.

♪ **S.C.:** Right. Ralph Gleason, when the Who first played at the Monterey Pop Festival, referred to "the same cheap guitar and the same cheap amp that Townshend would rap across the front of the grill, then hit his guitar against it," and I found it kinda strange because I knew that it was live equipment. I knew it was real, and I couldn't figure out where this guy got off tone saying that it wasn't real.

WINTERLAND: FRIDAY, FEBRUARY 23, 1968; A STORY IN PHOTOS

B.M.: And Bob Pridden used to leap into the audience and retrieve the pieces of the guitar; Pete would snap off a plaquette, and the plaquette would pop down in the audience, and it was Pridden's stuff to go and get it. This was a sort of a game with the band; he couldn't come back up and say, "I'm sorry; there were 300,000 screaming people and they wouldn't let me have it back!" He had to show up with those pieces of equipment, or the band was really on his case.

S.C.: Do you know whether or not there was any kind of kickback on his, on some of the more totally destructed stuff?

B.M.: To my knowledge, what he did in those days was he scoured music stores for bargains on good instruments like old Les Pauls, old things where could in fact justify the destruction of them. To my knowledge, Jimi Hendrix had an agreement with Fender; I know for a fact they provided white Stratocasters, [but] whether he bought them or [they] were given to him I don't know, but I know for a fact now, working for Gibson, that no such agreement ever existed and that Pete bought all his instruments himself, and that's really why, from my standpoint, he's rather not difficult, but I really have to come up to his ideological goals as regards the Gibson products. He has always bought them, and it's even easier for him to buy them now.

S.C.: Could you briefly explain some of the needs that they have gone through, that you were associated with, some specific needs, like problems that Entwistle was having in bass reproduction and different usages of speakers and speaker configurations and things?

B.M.: At the time that we dealt with the Who, the one unique thing about them as a very contemporary, fast-breaking band changing the face of American music, from certain music to what they were doing, was that Entwistle was interested in the amps that Sunn built for guitar players. Sunn built an amp that had a 15-inch speaker on the bottom and a high-frequency horn and driver on the top, and it didn't produce any midrange. At the time that we were working together, the artists' advisory board for Sunn were the Buffalo Springfield, who were pitching 12-by-12-inch speakers and midrange reproduction, and the Who and Hendrix, and it amazed us that John Entwistle sorted through the Sunn line and disregarded our positioning of the unit as a lead guitar amp and found that it gave him some highs that he couldn't get with any other unit. At that time, there were no real speaker cabinets in the market with high quality—this is a JBL special-designed, high-frequency horn as opposed to tiny little . . . I won't mention the name! It was harder for Sunn to meet Peter's needs as quickly as Peter needed. Peter was definitely a foremost proponent of 4 × 12 speaker cabinets—12-inch speakers and a cabinet, and a squared cabinet, but he wasn't really locked into any specific horn enclosure. I am not positive, but I think that he at that time specified Celestion speakers.

S.C.: I have heard that at that time when they were using those big Marshall cabinets, it was actually the Who that said to Jim Marshall, "Cut it in half," because it would be better on the road.

B.M.: Yeah, I remember them telling me that. Their relationship with me had in large part to do with things they had already told Jim Marshall.

S.C.: What can you explain to me about Peter's and John's guitar needs?

B.M.: Right now, John Entwistle is working in collaboration with the research-and-development division of the Gibson guitar company to give us his view of a second-generation electric bass guitar. He's interested in internal preamp and that sort of thing. His general overview of the market and of the needs of the player across the board is that the player is interested primarily in the electronic sophistication. He is using Alembic instruments, but he really thinks that Alembic is making a mistake in spending the money and the time in the woods, where it's his feeling that where they really capture their instruments is in the preamplifiers, and therefore, he's trying to make Gibson aware of their progress. Among the people that I've dealt with, John is the most active designer of musical instruments. In other words, he came very early to an awareness that he was learning how to play an instrument that he was designing as he was learning how to play it. Most people in the business who know John have heard John's explanation of going into the piano string company, sitting down half a day, and, at the end of the day, giving them their main string, which is now standard among players, including Stanley Clarke.

S.C.: Yeah, that was the Rotosound design. Is Rotosound originally a piano string manufacturer?

B.M.: It was a piano string manufacturer and a manufacturer of medical implements, precision wire winding.

S.C.: I always noticed that too in the early Who sound in the way that Entwistle was running his bass. The tone of his strings reminded me very much of the piano, with that ring and resonance, and plus he would get all that top end through his amplification system.

🎵 **B.M.:** He's really into the rusty sound; his biggest influence as a young player was Duane Eddy, that rusty, twangy sound. My feeling in observing him over this period of time is that I think he is still pursuing the same goals soundwise. He's just more sophisticated, being exposed to more technology. Peter I would say the same thing about, that he basically is pursuing the same sound, he is only more into sound reinforcement, which takes you into a whole other area of technology.

🎵 **S.C.:** Can you explain to me some of the speaker problems they were running across not only at the destruction part of it, but, say, volume destruction? For instance, on the *Live at Leeds* album there is a part, and I believe it's in "My Generation," when you can actually hear it's either a speaker breaking up or something but it's flapping quite badly, and I was wondering whether or not he had any specific problems with speaker usage and his volume control.

🎵 **B.M.:** He had more problems with some speakers than he did with others. I think he experimented with speakers frequently because of the fact that he was a volume player. He did definitely always have problems with speakers, because he was in need of a tremendous amount of volume. The area that Peter is interested in, as regards Gibson and the area that Gibson is responding him on, is the area of quality control.

🎵 **S.C.:** I noticed in a shot, in fact I looked at some this morning that Chuck Boyd took at the time you were with Pete in Portland, [that] he was pointing to the neck, and I was wondering if he has any neck preferences or customizing features . . .

🎵 **B.M.:** From the standard available instrument now, he likes to take the back down. He likes room between his palm and the neck, and in those pictures, he was explaining that he had had that neck brought down, and then it became unstable because of the quality of the wood. [Tape skips] Pete uses Gibson 340 strings and he uses two B strings. He pulls out the G string. And John Entwistle probably plays with the lowest action on a bass ever done, and this is a quote from Rick Turner of Alembic and from Bruce Bolan at Gibson!

🎵 **S.C.:** No kidding! You mentioned Alan Rogan, who is Pete's guitar man.

🎵 **B.M.:** He is personally responsible for setting up Peter's instruments. At this point, Peter doesn't even take up an instrument until it's set up with his particular setup.

🎵 **S.C.:** You mentioned something to me the other day on the phone about some bridges you were talking to Pete Townshend about—some bridge replacements or something of that nature.

🎵 **B.M.:** Yeah, he prefers the new shallow-style Gibson bridge. Most bridges in stock around the world are the old style, and this is a Gibson improvement. He's unable to get those as spare parts, so I had to get him some.

🎵 **S.C.:** Back then, for a while, Pete was using ES-335 (although it was very short lived); he also used some Strats early on, and then all of a sudden he got into the SGs, and I read somewhere where he was saying that he really dug the old SGs because their necks were soft and he could bend them and physically manipulate the instrument to achieve musical statements, plus leaping about the stage (you know, the guy is almost a ballet dancer and an athlete), and seems to me that SGs are very light guitars and you can be quite mobile with them, but on the other hand, you look at a Les Paul, which is quite heavy; does he see any problems in that relationship?

🎵 **B.M.:** No, I would say that there was probably more to do with humbucker pickups than any other single thing as to the use of the SG. That's just a guess on my part, but it's based on the fact that now he is experimenting with the use of the DiMarzio pickups in his Les Pauls. He's dropping one in the middle now . . . or, actually, I take it back: John Entwistle says that Peter throws it in there just to get more happening, and he's not interested in that particular pickup or anything; it's just that he likes the humbucker and super humbucker-type thing. What's interesting in my relationship here is that I was traveling with two people: Jimi Hendrix on one hand and the Who on the other, and they were all in the same label in England and handled essentially by the same people. There are a lot of people that intimated that Jimi was doing what he had seen Pete Townshend do, and Pete Townshend was . . . I won't say he was defensive about that—he was above the issue, but when he was taking exception with the phenomenon of Jimi Hendrix, I got the feeling that he was taking exception with the act as opposed to what he was really doing. You know, picking your guitar with your teeth, jumping around, because Peter was the premier doer of that.

John and Keith in San Francisco on Friday, February 23, before their first Winterland appearance. A couple of the photos Douglas Kent Hall took on that day were used for Sunn equipment advertisements. *Courtesy of Dawn Hall Estate of Douglas Kent Hall; scans from original negatives preserved at Princeton University Library*

John and Keith in San Francisco on Friday, February 23, before their first Winterland appearance. A couple of the photos Douglas Kent Hall took on that day were used for Sunn equipment advertisements. *Courtesy of Dawn Hall Estate of Douglas Kent Hall; thanks to Princeton University Library*

WINTERLAND DRESSING ROOM,
BEFORE FIRST SET

Photographs this page bottom to page 83 by Frank Zinn (courtesy of Richard Martin Frost); photos pages 84 to 89 courtesy of Dawn Hall Estate of Douglas Kent Hall; scans from original negatives preserved at Princeton University Library

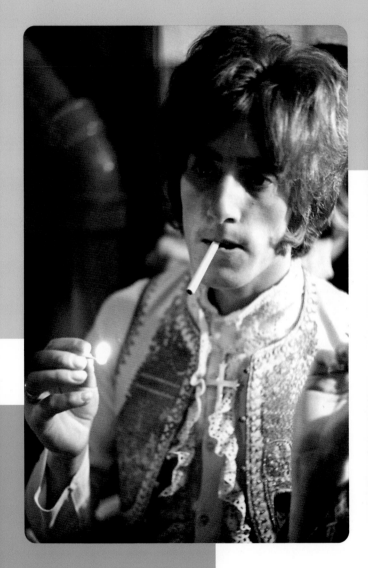

WINTERLAND: FRIDAY, FEBRUARY 23, 1968; A STORY IN PHOTOS

WINTERLAND: FRIDAY, FEBRUARY 23, 1968; A STORY IN PHOTOS

All photos courtesy of Dawn Hall Estate of Douglas Kent Hall (scans from original negatives preserved at Princeton University Library), except photographs on top page 111, page 112 and 114–115 by Frank Zinn (courtesy of Richard Martin Frost)

WINTERLAND: FRIDAY, FEBRUARY 23, 1968; A STORY IN PHOTOS

91

WINTERLAND: FRIDAY, FEBRUARY 23, 1968; A STORY IN PHOTOS

TEENAGE WASTELAND

WINTERLAND: FRIDAY, FEBRUARY 23, 1968; A STORY IN PHOTOS

WINTERLAND: FRIDAY, FEBRUARY 23, 1968; A STORY IN PHOTOS

97

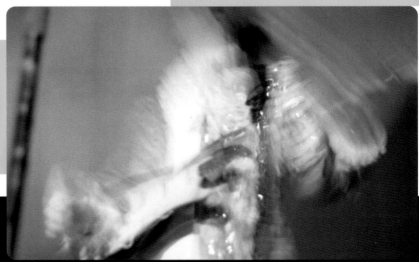

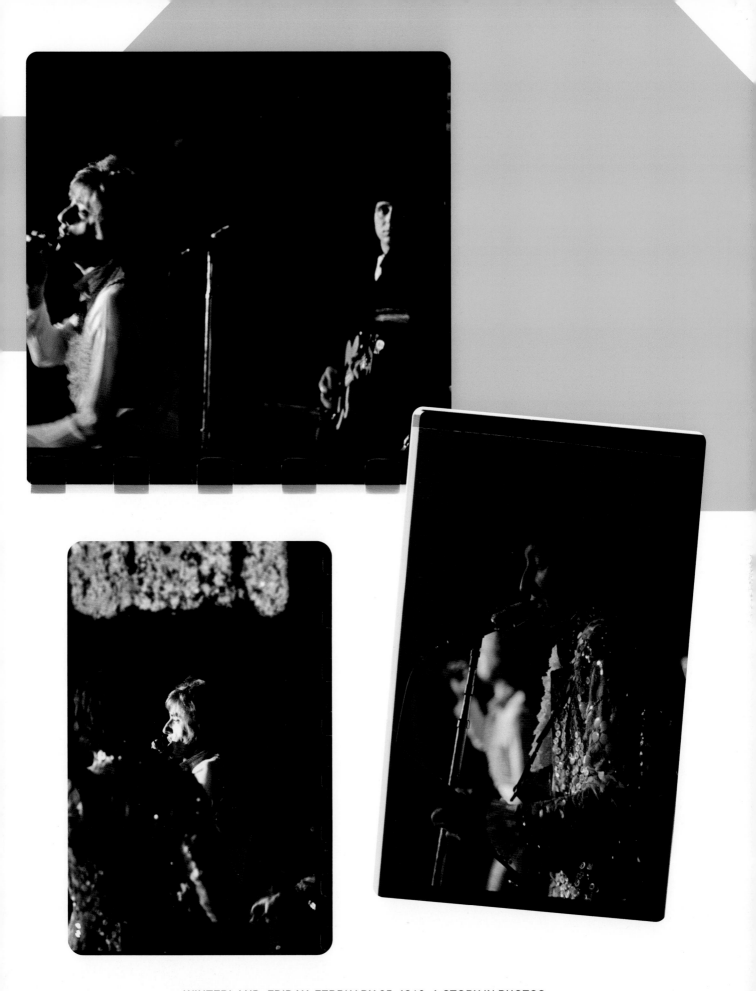

WINTERLAND: FRIDAY, FEBRUARY 23, 1968; A STORY IN PHOTOS

TEENAGE WASTELAND

WINTERLAND: FRIDAY, FEBRUARY 23, 1968; A STORY IN PHOTOS

105

TEENAGE WASTELAND

WINTERLAND: FRIDAY, FEBRUARY 23, 1968; A STORY IN PHOTOS

107

TEENAGE WASTELAND

WINTERLAND: FRIDAY, FEBRUARY 23, 1968; A STORY IN PHOTOS

WINTERLAND DRESSING ROOM, GETTING READY
FOR SECOND SET

Photos courtesy of Dawn Hall Estate of Douglas Kent Hall; scans from original negatives preserved at Princeton University Library

All photos courtesy of Dawn Hall Estate of Douglas Kent Hall; scans from original negatives preserved at Princeton University Library

WINTERLAND: FRIDAY, FEBRUARY 23, 1968; A STORY IN PHOTOS

119

TEENAGE WASTELAND

WINTERLAND: FRIDAY, FEBRUARY 23, 1968; A STORY IN PHOTOS

WINTERLAND: FRIDAY, FEBRUARY 23, 1968; A STORY IN PHOTOS

TEENAGE WASTELAND

TEENAGE WASTELAND

WINTERLAND: FRIDAY, FEBRUARY 23, 1968; A STORY IN PHOTOS

127

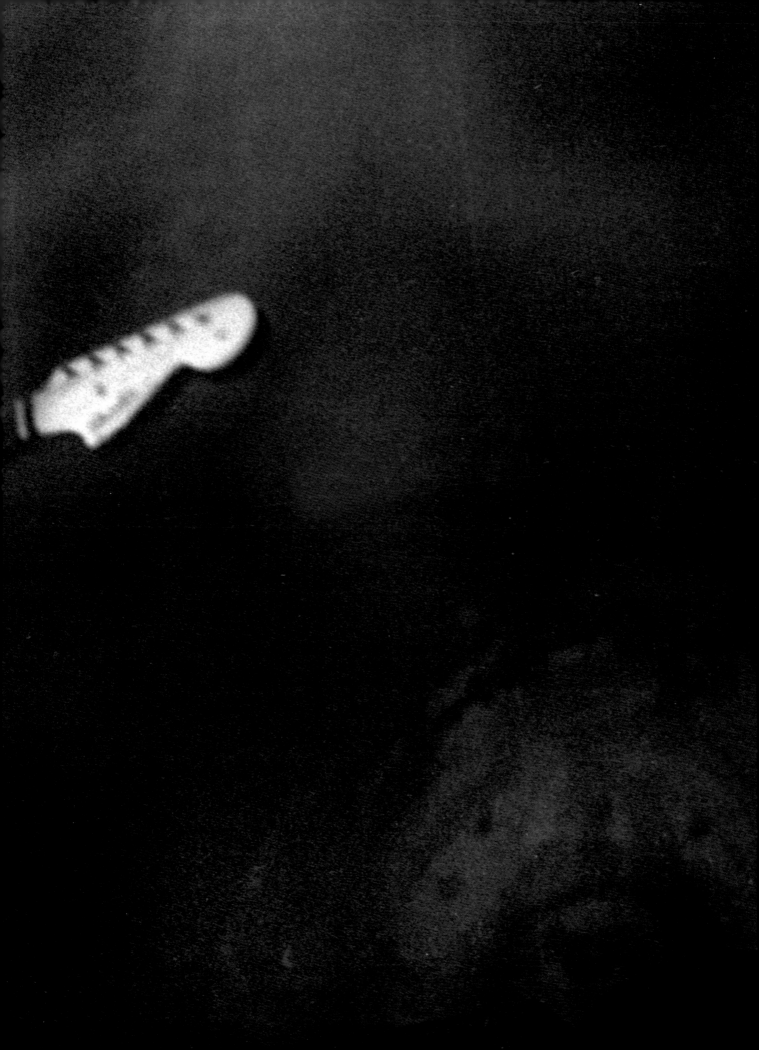

Pete chatting after the shows, before leaving
Winterland. *Photographs by Frank Zinn (courtesy
of Richard Martin Frost)*

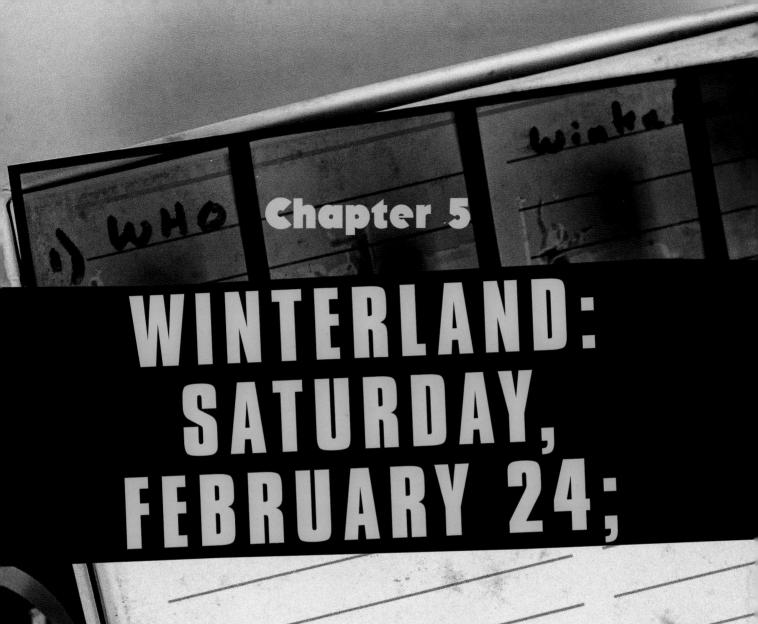

Chapter 5

WINTERLAND: SATURDAY, FEBRUARY 24;

A STORY IN PHOTOS

Hanging around San Francisco with photographer Jim Marshall in the morning of February 24, 1968, before the second appearance at Winterland. Marshall photographed the band for *Teen Set* magazine. © *Jim Marshall Photography LLC*

SET LIST*

FIRST SET:

"SUBSTITUTE"

"PICTURES OF LILY"

"SUMMERTIME BLUES"

"TATTOO"

"I'M A BOY"

"HAPPY JACK"

"MY WAY (Easy Goin' Guy)"

"A QUICK ONE, WHILE HE'S AWAY"

SECOND SET:

"RUN RUN RUN"

"I CAN'T EXPLAIN"

"DON'T LOOK AWAY"

"BORIS THE SPIDER"

"RELAX"

"I CAN SEE FOR MILES"

"SHAKIN' ALL OVER"

"MY GENERATION"

Roger with ex–Ronette Veronica Bennett (later Ronnie Spector) in the Winterland dressing room on February 24, 1968. © Jim Marshall Photography LLC

Saturday night, February 24, was also special and full of highlights—if possible, even more memorable than the previous night, disturbed by the would-be-Abbie-Hoffman audience member. Two eyewitnesses in particular provide very interesting anecdotes regarding what happened before the performances and in between sets: the first person, who wishes to remain anonymous, claims to have seen as fill-in bass player for the Vagrants none other than Phil Spector, the legendary producer of hits such as the Ronettes' "Be My Baby," the Righteous Brothers' "You Lost that Loving Feeling," or Ike & Tina Turner's "River Deep – Mountain High," and inventor of the Wall of Sound arrangement formula, which all the songs he produced carry as his distinctive trademark.

Although the original Vagrants' bass player Larry West denies Phil Spector taking over for him at Winterland on February 24, 1968, a photo by Jim Marshall taken in the dressing room and showing ex-Ronette Veronica "Ronnie" Bennett (later Spector) next to Roger Daltrey confirms the presence of Phil Spector that night anyway: at that time, Phil and Ronnie were living in Beverly Hills, Los Angeles, leading a toxic relationship based on the complete control of the producer over Ronnie's life. His well-known possessive and paranoid personality would very rarely let the girl out alone, which explains how she couldn't have been with nobody but Phil Spector the night of February 24 at Winterland. The suffocating affair would only worsen after the couple's marriage a month and a half later, on April 14, after which Ronnie Bennett adopted the surname Spector.

As the anonymous source tells,

That was an interesting night. They were performing on the south side of the hall, the long side to the south, and the dressing rooms were on the right as one faced the stage. I sat over in the right-hand corner after the Who finished their first set. Leslie West and the Vagrants were there, and they were taking a break and sitting in the seats in front of me. Phil Spector happened to be playing with them. He used to bring musicians up from Los Angeles to back the performers on Tom Donahue's "Rocking at the Cow Palace" shows. He would play bass. That night, the seat I was sitting in was on the side of the hall across from the stage, toward the end of the hall opposite the entrance. It was below the balcony, an otherwise empty section where Phil Spector and Leslie West and one other person were sitting abreast of each other two rows down. Spector was bragging about getting down ten times the previous night with somebody, acting like he was full of crank. A friend of mine, Jim Beam, went down and knocked on the dressing-room door. The dressing room was at one end of the hall, while the stage was in the middle of the hall, with seats in back and no seats in front. There was no backstage for that stage. The performers had to walk along the edge of the hall and up some stairs to get to the stage. My friend joined the Who, drinking beer, and Keith Moon gave him a broken Zildjian cymbal from their earlier performance that night, and he took it home.[1]

Who wouldn't wish to be that guy Jim Beam for just one night, or at least to have been with him in the Winterland dressing room, hanging out with the Who in between sets? Those who weren't as lucky can now have the chance to see what Jim witnessed in the dressing room through the very special photos, and words, of another person who was there in that exact moment: Craig Patterson:

When the boys and I went to the Winterland show on February 24, it had been only three days since we saw the Who in San Jose. We were still recovering from *that* concert! Our friend Kevin Jarvis didn't go to this show with us, which was unusual, but we figured that he was still recovering from his successful rescue of his guitar from the clutches of Pete Townshend at the San Jose Civic gig.[2]

The Who were topping a bill that included the Vagrants, a New York band featuring Leslie West, who was unknown at this time. West was a hell of a

player, using a Gibson Les Paul Junior, which was dwarfed by his plus-size frame. The Vagrants were LOUD. Cannonball Adderley and his jazz band rounded out the bill. Bill Graham loved putting bands and solo musicians of very different genres together for his presentations. The man was a pioneer.

In June of 1969, Graham would pair up the Who with Woody Herman and the Herd, a "big band" from the forties.

We brought a chipboard guitar case with a beat-up acoustic guitar inside Winterland with us. My best friend, Randy Tinch, had dredged it up somewhere. We wanted to give it to Pete or, failing that, get his attention so I could get a shot of him looking at us so I could take some pictures of him with my trusty Kodak Instamatic. After all, this plan had worked at the San Jose show, and *this time* we were eager to give him the guitar AND let him keep it. We were allowed to bring the guitar into Winterland with absolutely no questions, or even a cursory examination. *This is how things were then* . . .

Scrambling through the lobby, we wound up sitting on the floor two "rows" back, on Pete's side of the stage. In those days, "festival seating" was still doable. When the band walked onstage for their first set, our plan was to wait a couple of songs and then offer to hand over the guitar (in its case) to

First set. *Photo taken by Craig Patterson*

Winterland dressing room, before the second set. Pete receiving the Kay acoustic guitar brought backstage for him by Randy Tinch and Craig Patterson. *Photos taken by Craig Patterson*

Pete and snap off a couple of pictures. However, we became starstruck when Pete looked down at us and didn't acknowledge the guitar or us.

The band played exceptionally well that night, and LOUD of course. Pete had his Marshall tops and four Sound City cabinets, with their ripped grill cloths. Right before the end of the set, Keith Moon got up from behind his Pictures of Lily drum kit with a medium-sized cymbal in one hand. He walked to the front of the stage between Pete and Roger and handed the cymbal to a bearded guy in the front row. Just like that. The crowd went "OOOOOOOH!!" When the set had ended, we still hadn't made a move to give Pete the guitar (however, I HAD fired off a couple of shots anyway). So the guy with the cymbal, whose name was Jim, saw our guitar case and said, "Do you want to give that to Pete?" We said, "Oh, yeah," so Randy and I followed Jim to the backstage curtain, where we were allowed inside. I recall being extremely nervous; this was unbelievable! We were pretty certain that we were going to be *discovered*, two teenage kids with a crappy guitar case between us, and be asked to leave. But that didn't happen . . .

The first person we encountered was Roger Daltrey. I offered him a Marlboro, and he took it. I nervously asked him what kind of cigarettes he smoked when he was home in England, and he smiled. "I roll me own," he said. We looked for Pete, but he was chatting with a journalist at the back of the room. I asked Roger where John was, and he said that he was roaming around behind the stage,

so we never wound up talking to him. Keith walked by and was sweating like crazy, chugging Coors beer, one in each hand. He took off his T-shirt and mopped himself off with it, as someone piped up with "He should have used Odorono!"

While we waited for Pete to finish with the journalist, Randy struck up a conversation with Leslie West, who was sitting in a folding chair just inside the entrance to the dressing room. "Where are you guys from?" Randy asked. "New York," West replied. Randy, a real wise guy, asked him, "Oh . . . are all the people from New York as fat as you?" Leslie just ignored us after that.

Pete was through talking with the journalist and sat down near us, next to Leslie West. I had my camera at the ready as Randy offered Pete the guitar case. "Pete, this is for you from my friend (indicating me) and me." He said, "Oh well . . . thank you . . . what kind of guitar is it?" as he was opening the latches on the case. Randy replied, "It's a Kay," and Pete said, "Well, you know, I've already got a Kay . . ." "Not like this one . . . ," said Randy. At this point, I took a beautiful picture of Randy, Pete, Leslie West, and the guy that got us backstage, Jim, looking in anticipation as Pete opened the case to reveal a beat-up Kay acoustic guitar. Pete gave us a little smile and said to Randy, "Yeah . . . you're right," and, *"Thanks, I needed another guitar case."* So that made us feel good.

WINTERLAND: SATURDAY, FEBRUARY 24; 1968; A STORY IN PHOTOS

Photos taken by Craig Patterson

We hung out for a few more minutes, and as we edged our way out of the backstage area, I found the nerve to ask Pete, "Can you do "Summertime Blues" again?" He said, "Oh, I'll have to ask John; he makes up the set list." When they came back out for their second set, Randy and I were back in our second-row "seats." Pete looked down at us and gave us a little nod, walked up to his microphone, and said, "We've had a request to repeat this one ... it's Eddie Cochran's 'Summertime Blues.'" I swear the band ripped into the song without so much as a count in. Request fulfilled ...

The term "I can die now" was made for moments like this.

Among all the uncertainties and confusion surrounding the band at that time, the positive vibes that welcomed the Who for their second time in San Francisco were a sign that suggested they were on the right path.

Craig Patterson's original negatives from February 24 and Steve Cowley's reel-
to-reel recording from February 23. *Photos by Stefano Domenichetti Carlini;*
items from author's archive

WINTERLAND: SATURDAY, FEBRUARY 24; 1968; A STORY IN PHOTOS

141

TEENAGE WASTELAND

15

KODAK SAFETY

WINTERLAND: SATURDAY, FEBRUARY 24; 1968; A STORY IN PHOTOS

143

Photos by Frank Stapleton

TEENAGE WASTELAND

Photos by Frank Stapleton

CANNONBALL ADDERLEY
QUINTET'S SET

WINTERLAND: SATURDAY, FEBRUARY 24; 1968; A STORY IN PHOTOS

ND SET

Photos by Frank Stapleton

WINTERLAND: SATURDAY, FEBRUARY 24; 1968; A STORY IN PHOTOS

151

Chapter 6
THE YEARS BETWEEN

Two 8 mm films of the Who at Berkeley Community Theater (June 16, 1970) and Winterland (March 28, 1976). *Courtesy of Sansara–Nirvana Murphy*

Only eight years separate the two Winterland performances of 1968 and 1976, a time lapse in which the Who attained a status they would have never foreseen back in the early days: after *The Who Sell Out* followed what is perceived by many as the "holy Trinity" of the band: *Tommy*, *Who's Next*, and *Quadrophenia*; there would be also one live album, *Live at Leeds*, and three compilation albums: *Magic Bus: The Who on Tour* in late 1968 only in the United States, *Direct Hits* in 1968 only in the UK, *Meaty Beaty Big & Bouncy* in 1971, the outtakes album *Odds & Sods* in 1974, and *The Story of The Who* only in the UK in 1976. Not bad for guys who hoped they died before getting old.

But is it really this easy to draw the band's success story? Most of the time, trying to draw a coherent, linear path of a band's changes and evolution can be tricky, in that it can prove utopistic and misleading, since it can lead to overgeneralization and oversimplification of what are in fact complex and multilayered cause-effect concatenations, which turn out as everything but linear. Among the subtle changes the Who went through, however, a *fil rouge* can be traced crossing all of the band's career, which can well serve as a simplified but all the same indicative and reliable vision of the Who's evolution over the years: their live activity in the Bay Area. Their progression of shows there, between the interestingly palindromic and thus emblematic '67–'76 years' range, can be seen as a bar raising one appearance

after the other. Every concert simply exceeded the previous one, building to a progressive climax of anticipation and success that reached its apex with the Winterland shows of March 1976.

From this perspective, this is why, symbolically, the two Winterland performances of 1968 and 1976 can represent the alpha and omega of the Who—the two ideal pinnacles that separate the underground entity of the band from the title of undisputed gods of rock Olympus.

Those who were at Winterland in those two nights of March 1976 simply remember them as life-changing experiences. Hand notes on reel-to-reel recordings and Super 8 films I have found in my research read, for instance, "Love at first sight."

It clearly can't be a phenomenon that would explain itself only by analyzing the two 1976 nights alone, but it can be fleshed out only by looking at the process that led up to them. So, let's see how the anticipation built up to those two 1976 nights by reviewing the Who's appearances in San Francisco between the first and last Winterland nights. Let's go back to where we left the four guys.

In 1968, the future still looked bleak and uncertain for the Who. They were still stuck in a draining impasse that saw them, for most part of the year, out on the road touring the US twice as headliners, from February to April, and then from June to August, while in need to come up with a new album after *The Who Sell Out*. The live schedule was tight

Notice Paul Kantner (behind Bob Pridden and behind the amps, wearing glasses) and Spencer Dryden (in one photo appearing behind Pete's legs) of Jefferson Airplane. Shrine Exposition Hall, 665 West Jefferson Boulevard, Los Angeles. Saturday, June 29, 1968. *Photos by Craig Folkes, courtesy of the Folkes family*

and wearing, but necessarily so: the road was thought as the key to the band's survival, while Pete was setting the coordinates for the new Who album, jotting down notes in the notebook he had been carrying since the beginning of 1968. As of February 5, Pete had two main ideas for the new album: as he told John Gilliland, on one hand there was the intent to pursue the operatic path, surpassing the previous, still-experimental attempt with "A Quick One, While He's Away"; on the other hand was the possibility to make a normal album with the many new songs the Who had churned out of that highly productive period.[1] With the perspective of not seeing Pete's ideas for the new Who project come to fruition anytime soon, with the touring taking up most of the band's time, the year dragged by with a series of fill-in, fast-and-easy-selling possible album ideas that on one hand kept the band productive as ever, but also contributed to make their direction look even more uncertain than it effectively was: the first, planned by Kit Lambert for a July release and aimed to cash in on the Wimbledon championship, called *Who's for Tennis?*, among a few new songs, should have featured "Call Me Lightning" and "Magic Bus," two tracks demoed by Pete back in the "My Generation" days, as well as many outtakes from the *Sell Out* sessions.[2] Failing to come about, the *Tennis* idea was scrapped in favor of a new album idea, which should have been called *The Who's Greatest Flops*, a compilation about which very little is known, apart from what could be gathered from the band's stage banters from concerts during

the two 1968 US tours. At Winterland in February and at Fillmore West in August that year, it was heard, for instance, that the album should have featured a selection of the best alternate mixes of well-known songs, such as "I'm a Boy."[3]

The Who didn't even manage to make an album out of the recordings of their live appearance at Fillmore East in New York on April 5 and 6. The reason for this is directly connected to the failing of the *Greatest Flops* release: as we learn from Roger in an interview made by Michael Geary right after the two Fillmore East concerts,

I think this live thing will be mainly because we're going to bring out an album which is going to be *The Who's Greatest Flops*, which has got "Pictures of Lily" on it. . . . If we bring that out, then our live album will be the same because we play the same numbers on stage.[4]

When eventually *Greatest Flops* also flopped, with still no new record in sight, the US label Decca put out *Magic Bus: The Who on Tour*, while in the UK, Track Records released the complementary *Direct Hits*, both featuring songs released in the previous albums, as well as known singles and B sides.

With the summer US tour finally ended and two records in each country displaying already-issued material, outtakes, and B sides and only a couple of new songs, the band's artistic direction couldn't have looked more ambiguous.

The only hope was the album that Townshend had been working on since earlier that year. The Bay Area first learned about the new project through an interview between Pete and Sandy Darlington published inside the underground newspaper *San Francisco Express Times* on August 21 (issue 31), and then through a full-length transcription of a much longer interview made by Jann Wenner featured inside the issues 17 and 18 (September 14 and 28) of *Rolling Stone* magazine. It was on August 13, after the first of three nights of the Who at Bill Graham's new venue Fillmore West, inside the Carousel Ballroom building on 10 South Van Ness, San Francisco, that Pete gave his first interview for the newborn newspaper at *Rolling Stone* at editor Jann Wenner's apartment.[5] As Who fan Trisha Daly recalls, members of the

Jefferson Airplane were sitting on stage during the first night of the Who at Fillmore West,[6] and as Pete remembers in his autobiography, some were also present during the interview after the concert. The connection between Pete and the Airplane dates back to a couple of months earlier, when the Who played at the Shrine Exposition Hall, in Los Angeles, on June 29, and the Airplane happened to be in town, probably to record in studio. As Craig Folkes' newly discovered photos reveal, Airplane guitarist Paul Kantner and drummer Spencer Dryden were sitting on the Shrine stage during the Who's June 29 sets, and Pete might have invited to hang out with the Airplane next time the Who would play in San Francisco.

The occasion came when the Who headlined three nights at Fillmore West on August 13–15, opened by blues act Magic Sam and James Cotton. The band had grown considerably since their last appearance in town in February and presented a totally different outfit; they had abandoned the pop art image in favor of a more down-to-earth, hardworking attitude, presenting a longer and tighter set list featuring more rock-and-roll covers such as "Young Man Blues" and "Daddy Rolling Stone." The transformation of the Who was before everyone's eyes on those three nights. After the show, Pete went to Jann Wenner's home to give his Rolling Stone interview, and along came members of the Airplane and Jack Casady's friend Boz Scaggs, at the time guitarist in the Steve Miller Band.

The ideas coming out in that occasion as the first draft of the new Who project named *Deaf, Dumb & Blind Boy* eventually became *Tommy*.

The album was the result of the convergence of different aspects; it was triggered when Pete's artistic ambitions took

Fillmore West, 10 South Van Ness. Thursday, August 15, 1968. *Note*: Pete used the SG shown in the photo above for the song "Daddy Rolling Stone." *Photos by Paul Sommer*

a definitive turn thanks to the influence of Meher Baba's words and the West Coast audience's receptive attitude toward music performances. As early as the Who were born, Pete had been trying in many different ways to work on pop's potential, pushing its expressive boundaries to the limit and trying to break away from the standard hit-single form. One of the outputs of his experimentations was represented by "A Quick One, While He's Away," which also became known as "mini opera," and later by "Rael," another attempt by Townshend to combine musical languages. The innovative formula that these pieces of music had introduced to the pop world eventually grew in depth, thanks to the influence of Baba's mysticism, for one thing, but also from the awareness that Pete felt when the Who played in San Francisco. There, Pete realized he was walking the same spiritual path as pop audiences he met in California. Their consciousness-expanding tendency, which also evolved into an extremely acute receptiveness toward music performances, made Pete realize that audiences might have enjoyed more-structured albums, organic works with a story line, just like

Fillmore West. Thursday, June 19, 1969. *Photo by John Peden*

they were enjoying more-structured live shows. *Tommy* was the synthesis of all these inputs, and its multilayered, metaphorical structure, which was almost cryptic to some extent, proved—almost paradoxically—the key to its success: every generation up to this day has mirrored itself in the same arduous spiritual and experiential path that a sense-deprived boy had to undertake toward self-awareness, self-recognition, and self-acceptance. In Baba's words, to become "God-Realized." Telling the story of sensory deprivation as a symbol of our own everyday spiritual isolation, Pete had, maybe unwittingly, tapped into something that is still not exactly clear, but that was and still is residing down inside people's conscience.

Tommy was the album that kept the Who from breaking up, saving them financially and constituting a "page 2" in their story.

San Francisco is where *Tommy* got its West Coast premiere, with three legendary nights at Fillmore West on June 17–19, 1969. There, the Who did not play the complete version of their album, however, but just a "sensible, generous amount," like Pete said on the final night. Something both interesting and funny happened on the first night, when many of those who attended remember Pete cutting short the first set, apparently having come down with the flu, leading the proverbial ire of Bill Graham to fall on the dizzy guitarist. As it turns out, from a recent conversation with Pete's friend Rick Chapman,

> After Meher Baba dropped his body on January 31, 1969, Pete had yet to go to India to meet any of the *mandali* (the inner circle of disciples of Meher Baba) and see the *samadhi* (Baba's tomb-shrine and final resting place). We talked about his trying to squeeze a trip to India into his schedule following that San Francisco gig—I encouraged it strongly—and during the afternoon before the Fillmore West June 17 concert, I took Pete down to the Overseas Medical Center on Market Street in San Francisco to get the requisite shots—in those days you needed everything from hepatitis to cholera vaccinations before going to India. That night, during the concert, Bill Graham comes on about twenty or thirty minutes into the show and says, "I'm sorry; we've got to cut the show short. Pete got a vaccination today and can't continue." It was the cholera shot that did it, as it creates not only a strong flu-like reaction but also considerable arm soreness. You can imagine how I felt about that! But that was for a good cause . . .[7]

The Bay Area audiences would not get a complete live version of *Tommy* until the Who returned on June 15 and 16, 1970, and played Berkeley Community Theater. What the lucky attendees witnessed on those two nights promoted by Bill Graham was described as the best version of the Who ever seen onstage until then; "the finest two-hour concert of temporary music of their lives," as reported Philip Elwood, an avid fan of the Who writing for the *San Francisco Examiner*.[8] After having performed before 500,000 people at Woodstock, and having represented the most memorable act to ever play at Fillmore East in New York, with a week of *Tommy* performances on October 20–25, 1969, the Who's momentum survived word of mouth's transience and was solemnly immortalized for posterity with *Live at Leeds*, recorded in February, released in May, and described by Nik Cohn for the *New York Times* as "the best live rock album ever made."[9] At Berkeley, the Who proved what they had promised with *Leeds*.

Not only that, but they took their act even further: two new and never-heard-before songs were added in the set list and created great anticipation toward the next grandiose project Pete had embarked on, just one year after the release of *Tommy* and still on top of its wave of success. The songs "I Don't Even Know Myself" and "Water" were initially planned to be part of what history has proved to be Pete's most elaborate project: Life House.

The vision behind it was so ambitious that it could not be translated into a single, definitive form. On the contrary, like debris from a Big Bang, the numerous songs that had been written for it scattered all across the Who's career to come. For instance, songs such as "Relay" and "Join Together," written for Life House, eventually became independent singles in 1972, after having transmigrated into even another project called Rock Is Dead—Long Live Rock, which also never came to be. Even *Quadrophenia*'s cornerstone "Drowned" dates back to 1970, when the circle of songs of what would eventually be named Life House was written. Each Life House song shines to this day in its own light, like stars in the sky, each one telling its own story and simultaneously revealing glimpses of a much-wider universe behind and reflecting elements that refer to the wider vision they were initially part of. In its embryonic stage, Pete Townshend's follow-up to *Tommy* went through different working titles, *Bobby* and *Guitar Farm*, as well as changes in the plot, before finally reaching its most recognizable form when it was given the name Life House. Not only was it envisioned as a new rock opera: it should have also been a movie. Townshend had been deeply influenced by sociologist Marshall McLuhan and was perfectly aware of his theory according to which the medium corresponds to the message. Mass media, says McLuhan, are not neutral: their very structure affects the message's addressees and is more effective than the specific content they deliver. The idea for a movie was an

Berkeley Community Theater. 1930 Allston Way, Berkeley, California. Tuesday, June 16, 1970. *Photo by Paul Sommer*

extreme way, something completely different, in order to change something that in Pete's vision had almost become sterile, like a well with nearly no more water to draw from: the binomial of rock concerts and their audiences. Pete also felt a correspondence between the Who's and rock's current status: both were taking uncertain ways and seemed out of depth.

After the *Tommy* tours, the band fell into a gloomy, depressed limbo. Roger would remember that "we were never nearer to breaking up than we were three months ago. . . . It's just a desperation feeling":[10]

> We're in a quandary because rock is in a quandary; I felt that where the Who was at was very much a reflection of what's happening to rock and roll as a whole. . . . I felt we were beginning to cliché ourselves in so many different ways. . . . We were becoming less of a rock band and more of a circus act. I thought that we were capable of getting a film together and working on new formulas and things.[11]

A film should have been that element, that medium, that could shake down rock's rigid and saturated structure and finally get through to an audience that was losing touch with the live concert experience. But what was it that Pete was seeing happening at that time?:

> I thought that rock was failing at the moment to fully get through to its audiences.[12] You used to walk on stage and play the rock songs you'd written, and in our case, do the tricks you do—and the audience would feel what they were seeing was a reflection of their own selves, their moods and frustrations. Now the spread of the audience is so wide, the dynamics are getting so different, that the intensity of performance is getting less. At a Who concert today, you get the feeling that you're on stage two hours of your life, two hours of your day, and in that time, you've really got to cram in as much as intense *experience* as you can, as much reflection, and stimulation and invigoration and so on, and you've got to do it for every person in the audience. Rock

has developed an audience which is now somehow physically muted.[13]

This phenomenon had many causes, according to Pete:

There is for one, dope, which makes you much more of an observer than a doer. There is also the fact that rock intimidates its audiences in a very heavy-handed manner. It says: Look, we're going round the world and we're going to be in your town on February 24, 1971, and you better be there if you want to see us. And when we get there, we're going to do our thing for two hours and then we're going back to the hotel and die as far as you're concerned. If you miss it, hard luck. So, the audience comes there and they pay their money and they sit there. It's very much them coming to you. Whereas in fact to us is just the opposite. To us is a very big gesture to play. It's the most important thing in our lives to play. We get the most feedback from playing. And yet it seems to be a very artificial, contrived and intensely wrong situation. The audience come to see the rock ideology exist. They come to see you make rock-and-roll noises at the policemen in the front row. They come to see the rock-and-roll thing happen, but they don't feel part of it. What I can really feel is the whole physical frustration of not being able to dance, not being able to sing, and if you did you wouldn't hear yourself anyway. This whole physical muting leads to the tremendous encore explosion at the end which is the only physical experience that the audience gets.[14]

It is clear that the intense past two years taking *Tommy* all over the US gave Pete food for thought regarding the direction where rock and roll was going, along with its audiences and performers. It seems, from Pete's words, that in the wake of historic events such as Woodstock and Altamont, at the sunset of the sixties, rock-and-roll had only apparently revealed its full spectrum, and its zenith had still to be reached. According to Pete, the genre had provided many answers without asking essential questions. It still had not exhibited its full potential. The liberating and cathartic process reached at every rock-and-roll concert's climax is really only apparent, being in fact a sterile, mechanical ritual based on a top-down approach in which performers dictate a determinate way the audience should respond to. Catharsis— for the Greeks, that "purification" and "cleansing" feeling that follow the release of emotions—is only apparent: How can it really be possible, unless performers and audiences communicate on the same level? How can elevation really occur, until rock concerts provide a predetermined behavioral scheme to which audiences and performers know in advance how they are supposed to respond?

From this conceptual background, Pete developed the futuristic scenario for his Life House plot: the scene would be set in a heavily polluted England controlled by the "Grid," a degenerative declension of Power that feeds the population, through specific suits, with experiences that they wouldn't be able to live in the degenerate context that has become the outside, real world. Within this authoritative, repressive regime that forbids music, above other forms of expression, one rebel named Bobby manages to hack into the Grid and thus invite the population to leave their suits for joining him in a rock concert called the Life House. There, with the authorities about to intervene and suppress the event, the audience and the band manage to ascend to a superior experiential and spiritual level and be free at last. Such ascension, in Pete's idea, was generated by the audience and the band reproducing "the Note," the sound of the universe that we tend to re-create every time we go to a concert but never quite manage to attain. This limitation, according to Pete, is due to a subalternity between audience and performers that prevents a mutual influence from occurring. The rock-and-roll formula then needs to be rewritten. Pete's philosophical and theoretical references were deep: the "Note" may have been elaborated from the single "One Word" Meher Baba shall utter when he would break his silence; the mystic refers to it as something all persons and creatures will benefit from, "because all forms and words are from this Primal Sound or Original Word and are continuously connected with It and have their life from It; when It is uttered by me, It will reverberate in all people and creatures, and all will know that I have broken my Silence and have uttered that Sound or Word."[15] Behind the conception of the "Note" idea and Lifehouse in general, there was also Inayat Kahn's *The Mysticism of Sound and Music*, and the stimulating lectures Pete had attended as a young student: one at Ealing Art College, led by Roy Ascott, regarding the so-called Creative Feedback Experiment,[16] and the other regarding the illuminating use of synthesizers, at Winchester Art College. On these two occasions, Pete became aware of how the artist's creation, or performance, in the case of live concerts, could be radically affected, positively or negatively, by the audience's reaction. Albeit unconsciously, audience and performers are in constant communication, continuously sharing feedback and influencing one another. However, what remains missing in a performance that would otherwise put audience and performer on the same level, thus finally being able to reproduce "the Note," is the active involvement of the audience in the creative process. And here enter synthesizers: at Winchester Art College, Pete learned how synths could serve as the ideal instrument for the audience to gain an active part in the creative process, and to finally level the traditional top-down approach: synthesizers are accessible and allow a faithful reproduction of a great variety of instruments for those who are not musically knowledgeable.

Leaving it all on a theoretical level wouldn't have made much sense: Pete wanted the Life House to really take place. He had already proved—through the application of Metzger's autodestructive art theory, at almost every concert through the smashing of the guitar, and also through many interviews up to that point—that rock-and-roll was something he took with extreme seriousness. In early 1971, Pete identified the Young Vic Theatre in London as the appointed venue to reproduce the Life House concerts. The events, in the form of "workshops" in which the Who and the audience should have interacted musically, also had to be filmed: How could the experiment have an effect on society and really bring change if its happening could not be proved? "The idea was to get 2,000 people and keep them for six months in a theater with us," tells Pete; "the group would play to them and characters would emerge from them and eventually the group would play a very minor role."[17] The Young Vic theater experience would serve as a test bed for what, in Pete's opinion, would happen to the rock scene in the near future: Pete thought that the rock ritual like it was experienced since the Beatles was coming to an end; he could not even see the Who in five years serving as spokesmen for the new generation that was forming, for its new anxieties and frustrations. *Tommy* had immortalized the Who in a sixties image from which the band was struggling to part from. The involvement of the audience, through the Young Vic workshops and the new medium of the film, was aimed to investigate a new formula of rock theater and to identify a new superstar. That's what, in retrospect, can also be read behind the title of the final result of this gigantic project, *Who's Next*.

In the end, as a matter of fact, the Life House experiment was never pulled off, since everything seemed to start crumbling around it: the Young Vic workshops, unlike avant-gardist performances like they were initially envisioned, became conservative shows in which the Who cast aside the new songs and played only old hits. It was due both to limited availability of the theater and to a feeble reaction of the audience; Pete had refused to advertise the workshops since he trusted in a spontaneous involvement from the public. Pete thought that this new kind of setting of rock concerts could offer something the audience would realize they had unconsciously been waiting for, but it was not like that. "It don't really happen that way at all." Time was still immature for a thing like Life House. It was so much a forward-thinking idea that during the times Pete came back to it in the years to come, up until the beginning of the new century, it always felt fresh, and not something that was written in 1971, sounding as something of the ultimate embodiment of the seventies. The definitive nail in the Life House coffin at the time, furthermore, was the missing support of Pete's mentor Kit Lambert, who, on the contrary, rowed against the guitarist by trying to pursue the grandiose idea of a *Tommy* film, boycotting Life House in many ways. The idea of making a *Tommy* film dated back as far as summer 1969: at the Pop Proms at the Royal Albert Hall on July 5 that year, Pete explained to a journalist that proceedings for the realization of a *Tommy* feature film were underway; it would have been produced by Universal International and directed by Joseph Strick, who also directed *Ulysses* in 1967.[18] Eventually, as Pete explained in 1971 to journalist Chris Van Ness, the band lost interest, contrarily to Kit Lambert.[19] That's when the fellowship between guitarist and producer started to crumble. By 1971, Pete found himself alone, tangled up in frustration.

In the end, the task to testimony the great illusion that was Life House was given to only nine songs out of more than thirty that were written, chosen at random by sound engineer Glyn Johns.[20] The reference to the Life House vision, initially, however, was evident only to the Who: in the final album, named simply *Who's Next*, no mention was made of Pete's idea, and no liner notes were written; not even Life House's cornerstone song, "Pure and Easy," containing the reference the "Note" in us all, was included, and it was also soon discarded onstage. Like an ancient Roman monument, Life House was left to only nine beautiful songs, just like ruins, to tell hints and bits of a once-bigger scheme.

Surprisingly, though, giving up on the Life House vision made the Who gain something perhaps even more meaningful: lacking a concise and clear story line, *Who's Next* and its nine songs attained a suggestive power for the fact that they *evoked* and not straightforwardly *dictated* something, thus allowing the audiences to always see different things in them. This allowed, symbolically, each song in *Who's Next* being "rewritten" and resemanticized by each and every listener.

Thinking about it, Life House as Pete had envisioned it, with audiences taking over the direction of the concert and performing their own song, in fact happened every time a Who fan put on a *Who's Next* vinyl or went to a Who concert in 1971 and heard in songs such as "Baba O'Riley" or "Won't Get Fooled Again" *his* and *her* own version of the song.

Maybe, this was the closest to the original Life House idea that Pete ever got.

Although Pete's initial frustration and tragic unfolding of events led the band to overlook the chance to record the 1971 tours (after all, *Live at Leeds* had been released, and recording the fall-winter 1969 shows of *Tommy* had proved a grueling and, at the end, pointless task), luckily, two shows were professionally recorded of the *Who's Next* tour. Where could it have happened, if not in San Francisco?

On December 12 and 13, 1971, at the Civic Auditorium on Grove and Larkin Streets, the Who gave what attendees remember as the loudest and most-powerful concerts they had ever witnessed until then. The two concerts were the last of a thirteen-show program scheduled by Bill Graham for the fall-winter season of his productions, which started with Frank Zappa and the Mothers of Invention at Berkeley Community Theater. John L. Wasserman wrote enthusiastically about the two Who shows in the *San Francisco Examiner*:

> It is said that the Who played a rock-and-roll music concert here on Sunday and Monday nights at the Civic Auditorium. That is an understatement. The story on Sunday night, and probably Monday night, was the stuff with which time capsules are filled; or should be. Hysteria, violence, theater, and drama, primal impulses, sadism, self-flagellation, and blood lust were all present in an evening that ultimately as more rite than concert, more ritual than music.[21]

It was also said that for these two shows, the Who had sold more than the equivalent of the Oakland Coliseum's capacity five weeks in advance. The Who had hit the Bay Area like a tsunami from which there was no coming back, and no chance to recover from. For the past four years, since the band's first appearance at the Fillmore in 1967, the San Francisco audience was treated to a tour de force that saw the Who perform each year harder, louder, and better. "I am the king of rock and roll," shouted Pete before the Civic audience, wearing a crown—and rightly so: his frustration seemed to have dimmed, yielding to a light self-indulgence and irony printed on a big, liberating smile. But the hardworking musician wouldn't spend a single day resting on his laurels, even after the *Who's Next* tour had grossed around $65,000 and the album was the fastest-selling the band had produced; the press would immediately announce, on the contrary, that the Civic dates would be the only appearance of the Who at least until 1973, since the band had filming commitments to meet throughout 1972.

Pete hadn't given up on the idea to use film as the ultimate vehicle and medium to diffuse and amplify the new ideas for the Who. In Pete's new idea, film had to complement a double album that would celebrate the career of the band. The title, both programmatic and evocative, was Rock Is Dead—Long Live Rock. The comparison may sound bold, but

Civic Auditorium, 99 Grove Street. Monday, December 13, 1971. *Photos by Dave Hori*

Pete's necessity to celebrate the Who's myth might not have been so distant from filmmaker Leni Riefenstahl's intent to celebrate the ideology of the Nazi regime: from an aesthetic point of view, both Townshend and Riefenstahl saw cinema as a symptomatic and latent reflection of reality.[22] In the end, however, neither project was really pulled off, but Rock Is Dead's basic idea and its elements finally transmigrated in what would become what is considered by many the Who's finest and last great record, *Quadrophenia*.

Pete had come to terms with the fact that, since 1971, the Who were going through a hard time as a band; the group's heterogeneity and the internal diversity of each of the four members from one another, from being the band's unique trait and main engine, were becoming the cause of a close demise and imminent, fatal collision. Each musician was drifting apart, caught up in the respective ambitions and personal issues. In addition, the music scene was rapidly changing, and the Who needed a new vehicle to keep up with the new public. *Quadrophenia*, celebrating the roots of the Who by telling the story of the troubled mod Jimmy in the London of the early sixties, served at the same time as a way to bring the band back together and, through the sophisticated musical arrangements, make it a fundamental part of the changing scene. Although *Quadrophenia* stands now by many as the Who's most enduring and representative work, its release in late 1973 was gloomy and chaotic. Not even for this project, just like occurred with Life House, could Pete's usual genius be supported by the technical capabilities of the time. For one thing, Jimmy's personality, split into four antithetical moods, each one reflecting each band's member, could not be transposed into sound with the appointed quadraphonic technique; the multimedia ideas for stage representations of the new opera, consisting of a quadraphonic sound system and a backdrop for film

Cow Palace, 2600 Geneva Avenue, Daly City. Tuesday, November 20, 1973. *Photos below and first two groups from top on the following page by Dave Hori; group of three photos on bottom next page and photo on page 167 courtesy of Eric M. Seedman, photographer*

projections, which should have been carried and set up from one concert hall to another, had to level with time, logistic, and financial problems.

Rather than restoring the band's precarious internal balance, *Quadrophenia* was the ultimate nail in the Who's coffin: with the record company eager to cash in on the 1973 Christmas sales, one UK tour and autumn and winter tours in the US were scheduled before the album was even completed. The band was put into a mad rush to craft a new stage act. Rehearsals were sometimes delayed as Pete failed to prepare synthesizer tapes on time, leading to frustration boiling up to dangerous levels. The tense atmosphere climaxed with a proverbial tussle between Pete and Roger, with the vocalist decking the guitarist unconscious. The premises for the upcoming tours were not good. Quite predictably, the hasty organization, overburdened by a lack of familiarity of the audiences with the new album, had an absolutely ill-fated effect on the shows: Pete described the first UK date of the

tour, in Trentham Gardens, Stoke-on-Trent, as "bloody horrible"; in Newcastle, halfway through the show, in a twist of rage and frustration, Pete damaged the faulty backing tapes, attacked the amps, destroyed his guitar, and stormed backstage; in London, an unprecedented demand for tickets for the long-awaited return of the Who after two years met with a definitely unsuitable venue for the *Quadrophenia* show—the Lyceum. As a result, more than a dozen people fainted in the first row during the first concert.

Things didn't turn out any better on their new North American tour: the infamous show at the Cow Palace in San Francisco on November 20, 1973, saw Keith Moon, fueled with elephant tranquilizers and brandy, passing out during "Won't Get Fooled Again" and "Magic Bus" and being eventually replaced by the lucky fan Scot Halpin. The return of the Who in the Bay Area was definitely below the band's standards, which had been rising show after show since the Who's first appearance there in 1967.

"Substitute me for him": Keith freaking out before fainting definitely and being replaced by lucky fan Scot Halpin. *Photos by Dave Hori*

The demanding Bay Area audience would have to wait some more years for another album and tour. Every cloud has a silver lining, though: the new two-night appearances scheduled for March 1976, from a simple "makeup" return for the grim Cow Palace show, turned out as a triumphant return of the Who in a totally brand-new outfit, promoting a totally different album than *Quadrophenia* and from anything the band had produced to that point, inside a familiar yet never-so-different venue from the first time the Who played there: Winterland. That homely place, hosting the old and new generation listening to old and new songs of the Who, formed a parallel dimension where band and fans were "captive in the carousel of time," like Joni Mitchell sang.

Many who were there would remember it as the most memorable concerts ever; history would mark it as the last great concerts with Keith.

Chapter 7

1975–1976

Although *Who's Next* and *Quadrophenia* took the Who to another, superior level of recognition since *Tommy*, being widely welcomed and regarded as the band's finest albums to this day, their making amplified dynamics that had been generated since the *Tommy* tour, which were constantly proving deteriorating to the Who. The band would have to confront these factors sooner or later. There were both private and also structural aspects undermining the balance of the band and of each individual. Most of all, there was Pete's primal fear, which he had tried to avert through Life House, that the Who could become a caricature of themselves, and that they could embalm themselves in their sixties' image, becoming the Chuck Berrys of the sixties, perpetually acting out their past.[1]

The stage, favored dimension for the band since the early days, turned out to be the context in which Pete's nightmare was always materializing itself more and more, year after year.

As longtime fan and music critic Nik Cohn wrote,

> By this time the Who's live performances have become almost an act of sacrament. They have been together so long, played so many shows, that their every move is now hallowed, takes on the weight of a litany. When Pete Townshend leaps high and descends in the splits, or Roger Daltrey whirls his microphone cord like a lariat, or Keith Moon destroys his drum kit, these are no longer mere gestures, a bit of casual choreography on the side. Over the years they have become observances which belong as much to the audience, the massed celebrants, as to the group itself. Indeed, at the climax of *Tommy*, when the lights go up and the crowd rises, 30,000 disciples made one, it is they who are the true performers, themselves whom they worship. "We're just middlemen," as Townshend has said. "The energy starts and ends in them; all we do is transmit it."[2]

Yet, somehow, even the greatest phenomenon in rock, which is the Who, by 1974 seemed to have lost its aura. Pete came to terms with the undeniable evidence of the loss of the band's spontaneity on the Madison Square Garden stage that same year: as always Nik Cohn wrote in another article,

When last Pete passed through New York, he felt that the group might well collapse altogether. He no longer knew if he could play, perform on a rock[-]and[-]roll stage. The Madison Square Garden shows were the worst he'd ever done, so humiliating that he'd been hiding ever since. "In all the years I'd been with the Who, I'd never once had to force myself," he said. "All the leaping about and guitar smashing, even though I'd done it a thousand times, it was always totally natural. And then, on the first night at the Garden, I suddenly lost it. I didn't know what I was doing there, stuck up on stage, in front of all these people. I had no instinct left. I panicked. I was lost."[3]

In *Sounds*, Pete gives a bitter recollection of those shows at the Garden, which revealed so eye-opening for him:

> It really was dead awful. I don't think I've ever been so depressed in all my life. I felt like a complete caricature of myself. Quite difficult to do a concert without having to go through this thing of doing a representational flashback of the last ten years.[4]

While, to *Creem*, he stated,

> When we were gigging in this country at the early part of last year, I was thoroughly depressed. I honestly felt that the Who were going on stage every night and, for the sake of the die-hard fans, copying what the Who used to be.[5]

It was evident, however hard to accept, that the Who needed to change direction in order to stay afloat. They needed a brand-new start. What could have possibly gone wrong with the last three studio albums—three undeniable masterpieces? From a hypothetical evaluation, it is possible that a latent discordance subsisted between these albums' intentions and the *form* in which these intentions were expressed. The most blatant example for this is embodied by *Quadrophenia*, born as a vehicle to hold the band together and, at the same time, to create a spark in the new generation. This ultimately went the opposite way. It became evident that the scene had changed radically, demanding from music a more disillusioned, realistic, direct approach.

This was a very different scene from the sixties, which ended leaving a huge scar in youth's consciences. Drugs had a lot to do with this. Since LSD was made illegal in the fall of 1966, its perception and consumption started progressively to lose its innocent aura, and the social and cultural significance of the ritual of "getting high" took on a different meaning. From representing a pathway to a deeper understanding of the inner and outer world, psychedelics soon started to be perceived as a form of escapism, an always more intransigent shortcut from reality. In particular, the way that substances were subjected to chemical alterations around the end of the sixties redefined drugs' social and cultural role and function. Author Joel Selvin mentions, in this respect, the operation led by President Nixon's administration to "clamp down on PharmChem," a nonprofit Bay Area laboratory that tested street drug samples, leading chemists to radically change LSD compounds.[6] Substances such as strychnine, speed, or methamphetamine were added to intensify the trip, leading the audiences to experience psychotic effects and manifest dysfunctional reactions.[7] It almost looked like the ultimate surreptitious and minute strategy to wipe away the counterculture, intervening on its founding features to make its implosion look like a spontaneous, inevitable reaction. The unmistakable proof of such an operation was represented by the Rolling Stones' free concert at Altamont on December 6, 1969.

The idea of a free performance to crown the 1969 US tour of the Rolling Stones was conceived as a way to gain a favored place in a music world that had changed radically since their last time in the States, in 1965, and in which the band still had no part of. Financial and personal issues, including Brian Jones's drug conviction in 1967, which banned the Stones from touring the States, had kept the band back from the many and rapid changes that swept away the rock scene, from Monterey to Woodstock. When the general conditions looked more favorable for the Stones in 1969, everyone saw the possibility of a US winter tour as the ultimate opportunity to catch up and make up for the missed chances of the recent years. By 1969, San Francisco was the undisputed heartbeat of the counterculture, and its waves had reached the far coasts of England: the news of LSD-infused free concerts in parks attracted the Stones like Ulysses to the sirens. They daydreamed of Golden Gate Park while playing a candid version of it in Hyde Park that summer, but why fake San Francisco when you can have the real thing? The Stones broke on through to the other side, presuming to know what the other side looked like. Soon they found themselves with the free-concert myth up to their neck: what generated from informal conversation with West Coast exponents as a *possible* "grand finale" for the tour, the idea of a free concert became dutiful to the Stones after the harsh critique from the press for the tour ticket prices being too high—varying from $5.50 to $8.50. They found themselves in the position to "owe" something to their public and to prove the press wrong about their "greedy" attitude. Born as an ideal "Woodstock West," comprising the cream of the Bay Area scene and the Stones as headliners, the Altamont festival went down in history as the symbolic

Images from the Altamont free concert. Saturday, December 6, 1969.
Photos by Shigeto Murase

end of the sixties. In its hideous and sinister look, the ghostly Altamont Speedway was a racetrack in the middle of nowhere outside Livermore, on the edge of southern Alameda County, California, and worked as a perfectly iconic proscenium to the end of an era. The allegorical death of the sixties was caused by the actual death of attendee Meredith Hunter—the climax of a day of violence between the hot-tempered Hells Angels, recruited to keep the people off the stage, and an unusually turbulent and rowdy part of the crowd. The causes had been abducted to the poisonous acid that was distributed and shared by the 300,000 there. Sam Cutler, who worked as tour manager for the Stones' 1969 US gigs and would later become tour manager for the Grateful Dead, supports the theory that the drug-related incidents that occurred at Altamont, which also happened on a larger scale to the point of changing the face of the underground youth scene so radically, were not an accidental self-sabotage caused by an oversight from street LSD manufacturers, but something planned—a Trojan horse with the intent to infiltrate the underground fabric and to boycott it. Cutler's source for this theory is Ken Connell, also known as Goldfinger, a drug smuggler and ex-husband of Nicki Rudolph, who in 1969 was the fiancée of Grateful Dead manager Rock Scully. Cutler met Goldfinger in Los Angeles on November 8, 1969, when the Stones were to play at the Forum. A month later, knowledgeable and attentive insider that he was, Connell immediately acknowledged that Altamont wasn't the usual scene, starting from the view of strange-looking yellow pills being shared in the audience, and the presence of suspicious people. It didn't take much for Goldfinger to realize that those pale-yellow pills must have been the cause of the diffused psychotic reactions among the crowd, and that the suspicious figures must have been none other than federal officers and narcotics agents. Goldfinger was sure that narcotic agents distributed thousands of tablets of poisonous acid at Altamont. According to him, the pills in question contained around 1,600 grams of LSD and may have contained adulterants. There are several reasons they couldn't have been produced by the scene's manufacturers, and thus they could have been handed out only on purpose by outsiders: it was clear to Connell that those tablets had been pressed on a type of machine that was available only in the pharmacological industry; California underground chemists couldn't have had access to such a kind of machine because of its prohibitive cost and the fact that the federal antidrug agencies monitoring the production of such equipment would have known of any suspect purchase. In addition, underground chemists were very zealous about verifying the drug's purity and wouldn't have taken the risk to gain a bad reputation by releasing bad stuff. Sam Cutler's analysis through Ken Connell's theory, which also links with Selvin's, is that since Woodstock, the government feared for America's

and youth's moral rectitude being bent by the progressive emergence of the underground forces to the overground. The three days of peace and music that took place in August 1969 rang as an alarm bell to President Richard Nixon and to the FBI, which would be presided over by Edgar J. Hoover until his death in 1972, and together they would cooperate with the Bureau of Narcotics and Dangerous Drugs for producing badly crafted and dangerous acid to distribute at Altamont and contribute to the scene's neutralization. Since Woodstock, free gatherings had been seen by authorities as an expedient for pushers to mass-distribute their product, and Altamont was perceived as the ultimate threat to the system.[8] The youth counterculture could have had its vendetta when a year later, in 1970, Grace Slick of Jefferson Airplane attempted to spike President Nixon with LSD, but this never succeeded.[9] Mike Wiseman, careful witness of the societal and cultural shift discussed before, was at Altamont, where he saw a fracture in the youth movement taking place: "I had a lot of friends who didn't get through the sixties," he says. "A lot of them overdosed from drugs or got hepatitis C or drank themselves to death. I feel very fortunate not to have had the same thing happen to myself. The sixties lifestyle led some people into some dangerous places. We still have a meth epidemic here in California, and that had a lot to do with it. In 1969, the East Coast was still into peace and love, hallucinogenics, and weed. That all changed in the fall of 1967 in the Bay Area. That had everything to do with the Rolling Stones' miscalculation about Altamont. I was there: the crowd was a monster because we had already gotten into that and there was no turning back. In my opinion, the Hells Angels saved a lot of lives because if they wouldn't have been there and if they'd had regular security guards, they would have been overrun by the crowd, and hundreds of people would have died. The Bay Area was a very bad scene in 1969 and even for

a year before that. Organizers often take the blame, but it never would have happened without somebody getting hurt the way the audience was, no matter how well it had been organized. It wasn't the organizers—it was *us*."[10]

Seeing what the sixties had become, it is almost automatic to think of what Tommy had experienced; although he was not the messiah, what he foresaw was very prophetic: audiences ended up acting like Tommy's followers in his Holiday Camp, asking for shortcuts from their problems. Meher Baba was right when he said that drugs constitute only a subtle escape from the conscious effort that eventually must be made;[11] the trip, in the end, proved "a delusion within illusion." The artistic output that generated from the sixties was grandiose, but in the end, when everyone woke up and succumbed to reality, realizing the dream was over, music remained a reflection of that dream, but not a reflection of its audiences and listeners anymore. It was a brave, audacious creation that had left their audiences behind, sober, and apathetic. The "teenage wasteland" that Pete sings in "Baba O'Riley" almost comes to mind. Although that notion, as Pete clarified, refers to the polluted England in which the Life House story sets, and should be read on an ecological level to reflect on the missed opportunities for a generation to protect the environment, it has been thought for years by many as an ideal, metaphorical portrait of late-sixties and early seventies audiences—like a boundless land of lost children—like Mark d'Ercole suggests in the book's preface.

Ultimately, the simple, basic, and direct repertoire is the only one that survived and outlived the sixties and was the only kind of repertoire the audiences could still relate to.

Quadrophenia was an perhaps too-multilayered, and too-sought-after operation to really be able to get through to a new kind of audience, like the Who hoped it could. Born as the ultimate bet to emotionally reinforce the band, the album couldn't help but highlight and amplify the fragmented nature of the Who, making them progressively look like a Townshend operation, with other three musicians acting like sidemen performing the songs he wrote. After all, it was Pete himself admitting that *Quadrophenia* stands as the work he is mostly proud of, because it's the result of his complete control over the album's production. Furthermore, a particular wording in the final liner notes inside the album, "Pete Townshend thanks the Who," looked almost like an ominous sign that the guitarist might have been progressively getting away from the rest of the band. This was eventually something he confirmed to people in the inner circle of the Who.[12]

But would quitting the Who really have solved Pete's problem?

On one hand, the band was obviously different than it used to be: in 1975, John had his own parallel band, the Ox, with which he could fulfill his hedonistic nature, living up to the most archetypal image of rock-and-roll star, touring and splashing out all his money; Keith wanted to retire in Los Angeles to start a regular acting career; Roger, soon after having personified Tommy in Ken Russell's cinematographic version of the opera, was already working on another film, always directed by Russell, this time about seventeenth-century Hungarian composer Franz Liszt, and had even won the ACB Interstate Theaters' New Star of the Year award, previously given only to actors of the caliber of Paul Newman, Steve McQueen, Warren Beatty, and Dustin Hoffman.

Yet, despite the centrifugal forces driving and pushing each musician to the edges of the Who, Roger, John, and Keith remained and would have always been, after all, the best interpreters of Pete's songs.

The first step for a new Who had to be the acknowledgment of the fact that the Who were not the same group as they used to be, but still, they were together: "The Who is much bigger than anything I could ever create on my own,"[13] declared Roger, despite the positive feedback he was getting from his new acting career. After all, it didn't take a *Tommy* film or *Lisztomania* to prove that Roger was a master of mimesis: he had proved it all along, since the birth of the Who, giving the best and most suitable voice to Pete's inner self.

If there was any future for the Who, it would become evident after the four musicians would regroup in April 1975 in a recording studio to listen to the vast number of new songs written by Pete—almost forty—pick out the best ones, record them, make an album, and take it on the road.

The press and fans everywhere waited with anticipation— and fear: "April 1975 is probably the most crucial month in the band's history. In fact, it is debatable whether there is a group called the Who as March 1975 draws to a close."[14]

The wait went on until October 3, 1975, when the Who's seventh studio album finally saw the light and took everyone by surprise: released simply as a single album, with no booklet, and no liner notes revealing sophisticated concepts or story lines, *The Who by Numbers* was the unexpectedly triumphant return of the Who after two years of frustrations and uncertainties. But Roger knew Pete well enough to be completely doubtful about the songs' impact and the album's positive reception: Pete is the living proof that frustration is food for the soul. As the faithful front man asserted, "Pete is a very mixed-up guy. You do need a lot of hang-ups and frustrations to do really good writing, and to me he is the best rock writer there has ever been."[15] Gone are the symbolic structures, the archetypes, the alter egos reigning in *Tommy* and *Quadrophenia*: what we see in *The Who by Numbers* is Pete in first person, coming to terms with his reality. Paradoxically, this new album is more Townshend centered than *Quadrophenia*, but what makes it step forward lies in its sincerity, straightforwardness, and sobriety. These are the keys that took the Who back to square one, to the freshness of the early days. On some respect, *By Numbers* sounds like a specular, symmetrical version of the *My Generation* album, with the same impetus, no more putting across teenage dilemmas, but a mature approach to the way things have become. We encounter the same naked, realistic emotions of ten years before, and no more of the self-consciousness and metafictional structure in *Quadrophenia*, hanging between first and third person; the pompous and baroque compositions, also, yield to the band's essential instrumentation, which does well without synthesizers and relies on the sole band's playing dynamics in order to get across Pete's private suffering, without artifice. In addition, contrary to Lifehouse / *Who's Next*, which were driven by inclusive and revolutionary tendencies, *By Numbers* embraces the more mature approach of introspection and self-examination. In this new period of Pete's writing, there is no reference to the outside context: "The chronic but contented outsider now has nothing to stand outside for. Lacking a macrocosm, the Who relinquish their value as microcosm. *By Numbers* is a Townshend solo album with the Who playing backup."[16]

Despite this, onstage the Who proved they were still *one*—the unity they have always been. Like Roger said, "I just don't feel I'm in a group unless we're playing on the road,"[17] and the tour promoting the new album would celebrate the new Who on the stage, looking and sounding miles apart from the worn-out, exhausted, traumatized band playing at Madison Square Garden the previous year. In fact, it wasn't until the Who hit the road again with the winter 1975 tour that their transition to a new group could be completely fulfilled: more than any other band, the Who needed their audiences to get on, and although not explicitly, their callout to their fans was ever so clear since the release of *By Numbers*—it only takes a look at the album cover: the unfinished drawing of the band made by John Entwistle, in the form of a connect-the-dots puzzle, might well be a way for the band to admit that the Who's identity can be completed only by its fans.

Roll I
The Who
27 March, 19
Winterland,
on Stage
may or other-
not, or
in color.

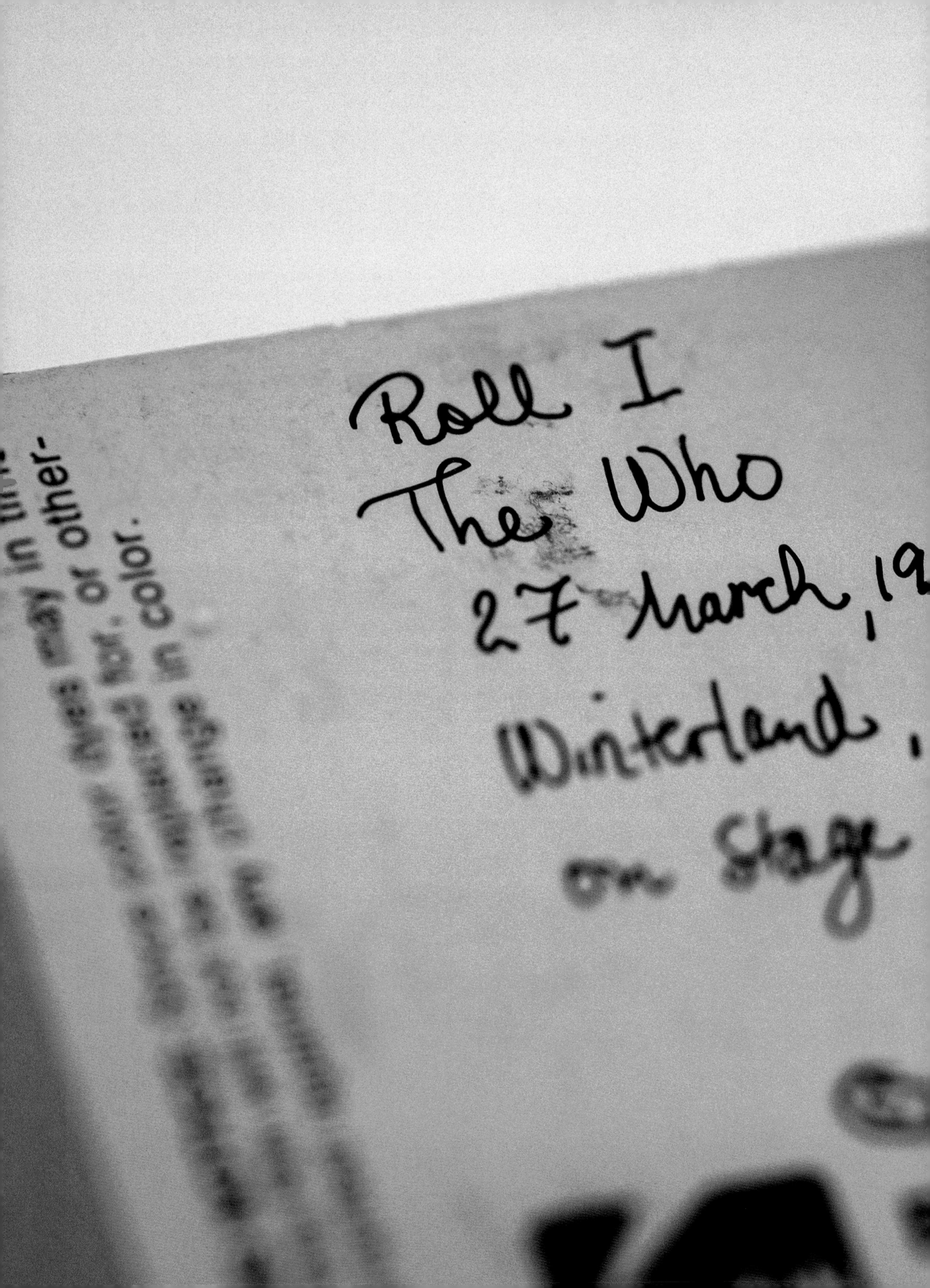

SAN FRANCISCO:

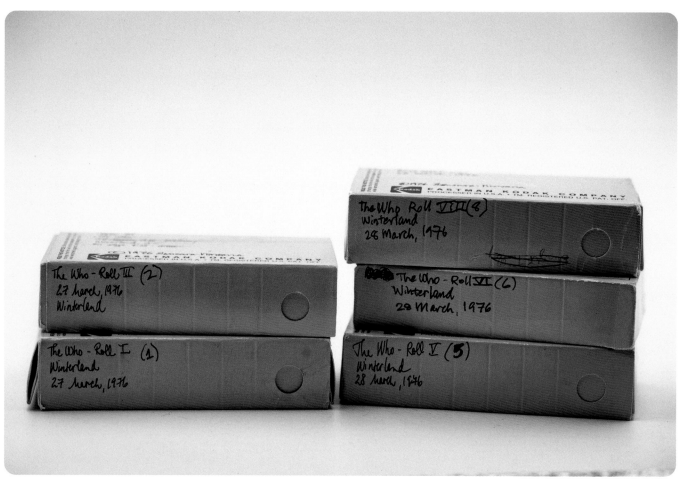

Original color slides and black-and-white negatives of photographer Sansara-Nirvana Murphy. *Photos by Stefano Domenichetti Carlini*

After eight years, one month, and four days, the Who made their second appearance at Winterland. It was their comeback in San Francisco after three years of absence since the infamous concert at the Cow Palace, and we would see how the announcement of the two new shows scheduled at the new Bill Graham venue caused a groundbreaking anticipation.

First rumors of the Who's return in San Francisco went out in December 1975:

> Although no contracts have been signed yet, it now appears that the Who will give two or three Bay Area concerts around the middle of March, probably at a smaller hall than might be expected, possibly even Winterland. The group is mindful of its last Bay Area performance—a debacle at the Cow Palace that saw drummer Keith Moon pass out twice on stage, while the band finished the show with a substitute drummer taken from the audience—and the relatively intimate local concerts are intended as a kind of make-up. The Who, incidentally, entered the Guinness Book of Records last weekend by performing indoors for 76,896 people at the new domed stadium in Pontiac, Michigan (home of the Detroit Lions at the time).[1]

Bill Graham's choice to book the band at Winterland was audacious: since the new tour's kickoff in October 1975, the Who had been playing multiple shows to sold-out audiences at UK venues such as Wembley, and in various stadiums across the US such as those in Chicago and Pontiac. Compared to the booking of the 50,000-seat venues, on average, that the Who played in their *By Numbers* tour so far, the choice for the 5,400-seat Winterland had something romantic and nostalgic in it, in that after all the other ballrooms in San Francisco had long been shut down, Winterland stood up as the last bastion of the sixties' music scene. The symbolic aura around those two March 1976 shows was strong also for this reason. Furthermore, Winterland was and would be in the months following the Who's appearances the backdrop of historic happenings in music: it was one of the selected venues where the classic *Frampton Comes Alive!* album was recorded, and where the Last Waltz took place—the farewell show of the Band, which took on the wider meaning of a celebration of the last ten years of music and counterculture. It almost becomes spontaneous to think "If those walls could talk . . ."

In the end, rumors made their way to the coveted official announcement: it suffices to know that it took only a single ad, published in the *Sunday Examiner* and in the *Chronicle* on February 22, 1976, to result in 43,000 applications for tickets to the Who shows scheduled for March 27 and 28. The official Bill Graham Presents poster, designed by the legendary artist Randy Tuten, featured mail-order ticket instructions, which are reproduced here:

Two tickets per order (no more, no less, and no choice of which show).

The ticket price is:

$8.50 per ticket

.60 per ticket service charge

.50 per order for return of tickets by certified mail

$18.70 TOTAL PER ORDER.

Mail $18.70 in a money order or cashier's check (no personal checks or cash) made payable to BASS (Bay Area Seating Service), to "The Who," c/o BASS, P.O. Box 57, Oakland, CA 94604.

You must also include a stamped self-addressed envelope for return mail.

Orders must be received no later than 12 Noon on Friday, February 27, 1976. Drawing of ticket receivers will take place on that day. The date of the postmark on your letter will not affect your chances of getting tickets. The tickets requests will be drawn at random. We are trying to give everyone an equal opportunity.

ANY ORDER THAT DOES NOT MEET THE ABOVE REQUIREMENTS WILL BE AUTOMATICALLY DISQUALIFIED.

Of all the 43,000 envelopes sent, only 5,000 were selected at random, and each of those lucky ones received a pair of tickets. The other 38,000 applicants received their $18.70 checks back uncashed. Yet, the *San Francisco Examiner* gave the chance to win six pairs of tickets for the opening March 27 show by mailing a form issued in an article dated March 4. "The Who could have sold 8 times as many," the *Examiner* article's title read.[2] Such premises made those two nights of March 27 and 28 make history even before happening, and set the right atmosphere for the perfect double-show appearance that no one in that old building would forget—not even the Who.

Among the lucky ones, there was artist and photographer Sansara-Nirvana Murphy, who documented both nights in black-and-white and color pictures, and the second night on Super 8 film. The effects of those shows on her impressed Bill Graham himself, who could not but relate to her words:

My journey with the Who started on the 18th of June 1967. I was 16 years old, and I fortuitously found myself amongst the hippies and the cool people wearing flowers in their hair at the Monterey International Pop Festival. I was there hoping that the Beatles would show up to play. But I found something that changed my life forever when the Who came on the stage. You see, as Pete wrote in a beautiful love song, "Now and then you see a soul and you fall in love . . . you can't do a thing about it . . ." I fell head over heels for the Who, and I was especially drawn to Pete. I couldn't get over how exciting they were to watch onstage, and there isn't anything like being engulfed in a flood of intense, spiritually explosive, expansive Who music. The Who at the Monterey International Pop Festival was far beyond anything I had ever experienced in my young life. And it was the beginning of an Amazing Journey to help me learn all I should know. Of course, at the time my journey with the Who started, I had no idea what was to come or where it would lead me. But from that day onward, I had joined together with the band. They became the soundtrack to my life and the springboard for my dreams. They shaped my desires, my ideas, my ideals, my view of the world, and my place in it. Like Pete Townshend, I became a Meher Baba lover. And I thoroughly love their sense of humor and their playfulness. They framed me inside my generation in such a clear way that I knew that I wanted my art to be a part of the big picture . . . and the music would help me bring forth my contribution . . . because there was magic in the music and the music set me free.

SAN FRANCISCO: MARCH 27 AND 28, 1976

Music in the San Francisco Bay Area in the 1960s, 1970s, and 1980s was addictive to many of us. We gathered together with our friends and smoked marijuana and spent endless hours listening to music blaring from speakers, and we took turns listening to music on two pairs of headphones. . . . We also sat on hilltops and dropped acid together overlooking the Pacific Ocean, watching the sun set, fascinated by how every molecule of the stony outcrop that we were perched on seemed alive and breathing, and we found ourselves feeling insignificant and small in a vast universe as the fog rolled in and blanketed us. It was a shared, spiritual, uplifting experience where music permeated everything we did together.

To this day, I can listen to a song by the Who and I am no longer alone in my room; I am hurtling through the universe guided by a child in a star, soaring through musical space and traveling like a rocket through time, immersed in the Who experience that is like no other—blending into and around the notes and crashing forward recklessly like a train smashing through barriers, dancing with abandonment, losing myself in a great overwhelming wave of sound and sensations, and remembering how great it was to be a part of something bigger than ourselves.

Many nights I would stay up all night painting my artwork while the music inspired me and made me forget me. When I heard that Bill Graham Presents were going to draw envelopes in a lottery type of system to decide which lucky fans were going to get to see the Who in March 1976, I decorated two envelopes with a Union Jack, guitars and drums, and Who song lyrics so my

entries would stand out and hopefully catch the eye of whoever was choosing from all of the submissions that had been sent in for the tickets' lottery. And my idea worked! I received tickets for both nights—the 27th and 28th of March 1976 for me and my friends! On the day of each concert, we got in line early so we had a chance to be up front since it was general admission. This was especially important to me because I wanted to take lots of photos!

I don't remember too many specifics about the two concerts . . . More of a general feeling of how awesome and intense the shows were. I remember being in line (I am not sure which day it was—whether it was the 27th or 28th), and Bill Graham came around and talked to us as he did many of the fans gathered on the sidewalk around the building, and he asked things like what time we got in line, is this our first Who concert? I remember seeing him confiscate a bottle of alcohol that some guys were drinking while they were in line. I also remember a guy asking me about how to use a 35 mm camera because he had borrowed a camera from a friend and he didn't have any idea which settings to set the camera to. So, I showed him the settings that I had intended to use and I told him that the key to getting a good picture was to hold the camera still . . . which can be hard to do at a Who concert, especially up front, where it gets very crowded. And for me, since I love to dance to Who music during the concerts, I would dance and then suddenly stop, hold real still, take some pictures, and then get right back into dancing, then stop, take more pictures, and repeat! During one of the night's concerts, I remember Pete briefly getting upset at Bobby Pridden, their sound engineer, but now I can't remember what exactly Pete was upset about. Maybe it was because of some feedback he was getting that he didn't intend to create! I remember Pete yelling and flipping Bobby Pridden off—English style with two fingers, ha-ha!

In 1980 I got a job as an artist at Winterland Productions—a silkscreen T-shirt-printing company in San Francisco of which Bill Graham was part owner. Winterland Productions was started with the idea of creating and printing silkscreen T-shirts for the touring rock bands to sell at rock-and-roll concerts. After a couple of years of working there, I became co-art director. Occasionally Bill Graham used to wander into the art department when I would be there on my own late at night, working on artwork that I couldn't get enough time to work on during regular working hours because I was always being interrupted to bid jobs, check other artists' artwork before it went to the screen department to be burned onto the silkscreens, or having to hand out and explain artwork assignments to the other 15 very talented artists. Bill Graham would kind of mosey around looking at the posters and the artwork on the walls, and occasionally he would have something to say. Behind where I sat, I had pictures of the Who and the Beatles amongst other stuff . . . there was even an English street sign on the wall which said Ranelagh Drive (the street where Pete had a recording studio called Oceanic) that was stolen by a friend of a friend in the dark of night and given to me to take home as a souvenir from my trip to England. One of the times when Bill came into the art department, he was looking at all the stuff on the wall behind me, and he asked me, "So you like the Who?" I said, "Yes! I love the Who!" And he replied, "In my opinion, they are the best live band out there. I don't usually tell people my opinion on that because I don't want to upset anyone. But the Who far surpass all of the other bands when it comes to live concerts in quality and content and effort." And I replied, "I totally agree; they provide the most intense musical experience possible and give their all in every concert which I have ever seen them perform." He then replied, "The best concert that I have ever seen, and as you can imagine, I have seen thousands of them, was when they played Winterland in March of 1976. Did you happen to go to either of those two concerts?" To which I gleefully replied, "Yes! Both nights! And it was the most awesome two nights of musical ecstasy I have ever experienced! They were in top form, and the music was so intense that it encompassed you in such a way as to make you feel like you were leaving your body—somehow losing yourself and becoming the music exploding and thundering through space and beyond time!" Bill laughed and said, "That's the best description of what it is like to see the Who in concert that I have ever heard."

Over the years I have written quite a few letters to Pete Townshend, and he was gracious enough to write me quick notes back. One of the letters I received from Pete was written about a month after the two March 1976 Winterland concerts. And it turned out that Pete too thought that those two concerts were amongst the best that the Who had performed for years.

It has been my dream to create an album cover for the Who or a solo Pete Townshend recording. I have not achieved that goal yet! However, once upon a time Pete recruited me to design the storyboard for an animated film that was to be called *There Once Was a Note* that Pete had wanted to make, based on Avatar Meher Baba's book called *God Speaks* about the evolution and involution of consciousness. Pete paid my way for me to fly to and from New York City and for a two-week stay at the Mayflower Hotel near Central Park so I could meet with his crew that worked for him at Towser Tunes, and work out the details for the animated film that he was going to write the music for. About a year after the project was started, Pete decided to set aside the project when he went into rehab for a drinking problem. Unfortunately, the project never came to fruition . . . much to my disappointment! But to this day I still believe in the words he wrote: "We all know success when we all find our own dream and our love is enough to knock down any wall," and I hope to find a way to work with him on any project he may deem me worthy.

LONG LIVE ROCK . . . I need it every day![3]

There could be a million words to describe those Winterland shows—as many points of view and details as the many who were there. But there is probably a much-better and direct way that can give the idea of what happened, and that is through rare and never-seen-before sets of photos that scrupulously reconstruct those two magical nights.

SAN FRANCISCO: MARCH 27 AND 28, 1976

Chapter 9

WINTERLAND: SATURDAY, MARCH 27,

A STORY IN PHOTOS

1976

Original color slides of photographer Sansara–Nirvana Murphy.
Photo by Stefano Domenichetti Carlini

SET LIST*

"I CAN'T EXPLAIN"

"SUBSTITUTE"

"MY WIFE"

"BABA O'RILEY"

"SQUEEZE BOX"

BEHIND BLUE EYES"

"DREAMING FROM THE WAIST"

"MAGIC BUS"

"AMAZING JOURNEY"

"SPARKS"

"THE ACID QUEEN"

"FIDDLE ABOUT"

"PINBALL WIZARD"

"I'M FREE"

"TOMMY'S HOLIDAY CAMP"

"WE'RE NOT GONNA TAKE IT"

"SUMMERTIME BLUES"

"MY GENERATION"

"JOIN TOGETHER"`

"WON'T GET FOOLED AGAIN"

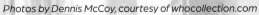
Photos by Dennis McCoy, courtesy of whocollection.com

WINTERLAND: SATURDAY, MARCH 27, 1976; A STORY IN PHOTOS

TEENAGE WASTELAND

WINTERLAND: SATURDAY, MARCH 27, 1976; A STORY IN PHOTOS

WINTERLAND: SATURDAY, MARCH 27, 1976; A STORY IN PHOTOS

191

TEENAGE WASTELAND

WINTERLAND: SATURDAY, MARCH 27, 1976; A STORY IN PHOTOS

WINTERLAND: SATURDAY, MARCH 27, 1976; A STORY IN PHOTOS

197

TEENAGE WASTELAND

200

WINTERLAND: SATURDAY, MARCH 27, 1976; A STORY IN PHOTOS

201

TEENAGE WASTELAND

WINTERLAND: SATURDAY, MARCH 27, 1976; A STORY IN PHOTOS

 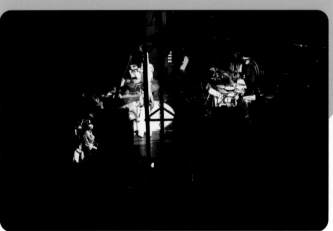

WINTERLAND: SATURDAY, MARCH 27, 1976; A STORY IN PHOTOS

WINTERLAND: SATURDAY, MARCH 27, 1976; A STORY IN PHOTOS

207

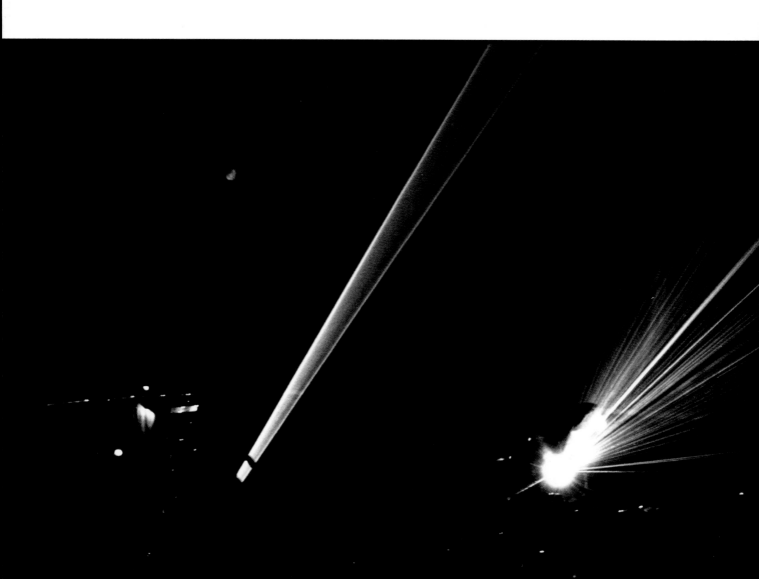

Photos by Sansara–Nirvana Murphy

Songs captured in this color film roll:

"I CAN'T EXPLAIN,"

"SUBSTITUTE,"

"MY WIFE,"

"BABA O'RILEY"

TEENAGE WASTELAND

WINTERLAND: SATURDAY, MARCH 27, 1976; A STORY IN PHOTOS

WINTERLAND: SATURDAY, MARCH 27, 1976; A STORY IN PHOTOS

Chapter 10

WINTERLAND: SUNDAY, MARCH 28,

A STORY IN PHOTOS

1976

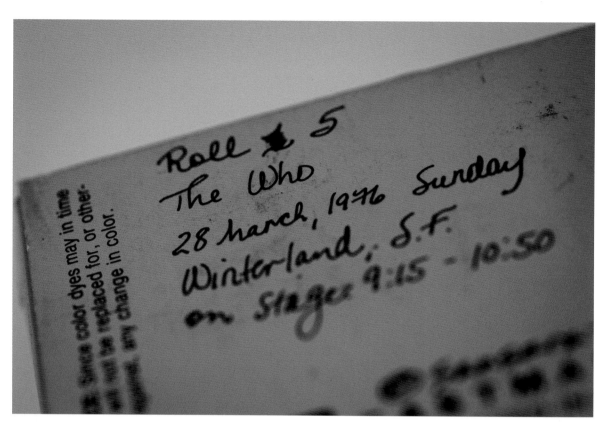

Original slides taken by Sansara–Nirvana Murphy.
Photo by Stefano Domenichetti Carlini

SET LIST*

"I CAN'T EXPLAIN"

"SUBSTITUTE"

"MY WIFE"

"BABA O'RILEY"

"SQUEEZE BOX"

"BEHIND BLUE EYES"

"DREAMING FROM THE WAIST"

"MAGIC BUS"

"AMAZING JOURNEY"

"SPARKS"

"THE ACID QUEEN"

"FIDDLE ABOUT"

"PINBALL WIZARD"

"I'M FREE"

"TOMMY'S HOLIDAY CAMP"

"WE'RE NOT GONNA TAKE IT"

"SUMMERTIME BLUES"

"MY GENERATION"

"JOIN TOGETHER"

"MY GENERATION BLUES"

"WON'T GET FOOLED AGAIN"

Opening act, the Steve Gibbons Band

Photos by Sansara–Nirvana Murphy

WINTERLAND: SUNDAY, MARCH 28, 1976; A STORY IN PHOTOS

TEENAGE WASTELAND

WINTERLAND: SUNDAY, MARCH 28, 1976; A STORY IN PHOTOS

WINTERLAND: SUNDAY, MARCH 28, 1976; A STORY IN PHOTOS

WINTERLAND: SUNDAY, MARCH 28, 1976; A STORY IN PHOTOS

233

TEENAGE WASTELAND

WINTERLAND: SUNDAY, MARCH 28, 1976; A STORY IN PHOTOS

235

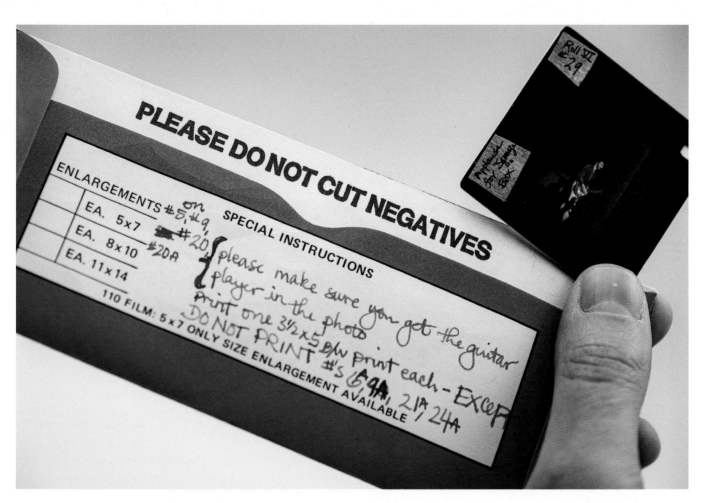

Photo by Stefano Domenichetti Carlini

TEENAGE WASTELAND

240

Photos by Jarid Scott Johnson

WINTERLAND: SUNDAY, MARCH 28, 1976; A STORY IN PHOTOS

247

Photos by Dave Hori

ENDNOTES

Introduction

1. Bruno Stein, "Roger Daltrey: Talkin' Bout My D-D-Dedication," *Creem*, January 1975.

2. John Gilliland, Pop Chronicles Interviews #112—Pete Townshend, audio recording, February 5, 1968, https://digital.library.unt.edu/ark:/67531/metadc1692078/, accessed January 15, 2023, University of North Texas Libraries, UNT Digital Library, crediting UNT Music Library.

3. Ibid.

4. Tony Palmer, *Born under a Bad Sign* (London: HarperCollins, 1970), 131.

5. Ibid., 132.

6. Ibid., 131–132.

7. Norman Mark, "The Who Come Up with Pure Rock Opera," *San Francisco Examiner*, Tuesday, June 17, 1969.

Chapter 1. That Motherland Feeling: The Who's First Time in San Francisco, June 1967

1. Various authors, "Regina to Get Look at 'Turned-On' Who," *Leader Post* (Regina, SK), June 29, 1968.

2. Loraine Alterman, "Just Be Patient! The Who Will Be Here," *Detroit Free Press*, April 7, 1967.

3. Molly Roth, "Break-Up Artists Smashing Success," *Shamokin News Dispatch*, January 6, 1968.

4. Bill Graham and Robert Greenfield, *Bill Graham Presents: My Life inside Rock and Out* (Boston: Da Capo, 2004), 189.

5. Edoardo Genzolini, *Cream: Clapton, Bruce & Baker Sitting on Top of the World: San Francisco, February–March 1968* (Atglen, PA: Schiffer, 2023), 45.

6. Mike Wiseman, communication with author, January 6, 2023.

7. Ibid.

8. Nicole Meldahl, "The Mysterious Death of the 'Mayor of the Fillmore,'" https://summerof.love/mysterious-death-mayor-fillmore/.

9. Graham and Greenfield, *Bill Graham Presents: My Life inside Rock and Out*, 200.

10. Paul Sommer, emails sent to author, December 20 and 25, 2022, and January 8 and 9, 2023.

11. Graham and Greenfield, *Bill Graham Presents: My Life inside Rock and Out*, 189.

12. Ibid., 220.

13. Gilliland, Pop Chronicles Interviews #112—Pete Townshend, audio recording, February 5, 1968.

14. Ngā Taonga Sound & Vision, *Peter Townshend*, RNZ collection, ID25183.

15. Ibid.

16. Conversation between Lou Adler and Donn Alan Pennebaker in Los Angeles, 2001, featured in the *Monterey Pop* Blu-ray box set (Criterion 2017).

17. Graham and Greenfield, *Bill Graham Presents: My Life inside Rock and Out*, 191.

Chapter 2. Summertime Blues, June–December 1967

1. Roy Carr, "The Punk as Godfather II—If the Glove Fits . . . Wear It!," *Creem*, October 1975.

2. Nik Cohn, "The Who: The Last of the Pop Groups," *Eye*, May 1968.

3. Ibid.

4. Carr, "The Punk as Godfather II—If the Glove Fits . . . Wear It!"

5. VJEOW, Dutch TV, John Peel interviews Pete Townshend, October 30, 1967.

6. Sonya Lopez, "Who Is Tommy?," *2nd House*, BBC 2 Color, Saturday, October 5, 9:10 p.m., and *Who's Who*, Radio 1 Stereo, 2:00 p.m.

7. Rick M. Chapman, email sent to author, January 31, 2023.

8. Rick M. Chapman, *Meher Baba—the Compassionate One* (Berkeley, CA: White Horse, 1987), 45.

9. Ibid., 17.

10. Ibid., 18–20.

11. Ibid., 12–13.

12. Ibid., 13–15.

13. Ibid., 29–30.

14. Ibid., 55.

15. Rick M. Chapman, *Bug Consciousness, Drug Consciousness & Flying Rug Consciousness (the Dope on Drugs—Pot, Peyote, Acid, and Beyond—from the Source of Truth)* (Berkeley, CA: White Horse, 2022), 59.

16. Ibid., 72.

17. Ibid., 43.

18. Ibid., 91–92.

19. Ibid., 96.

20. Ibid., 71.

Chapter 3. San Francisco: February 22, 23, and 24, 1968

1. Rick M. Chapman, email sent to author, January 31, 2023.

2. Graham and Greenfield, *Bill Graham Presents: My Life Inside Rock and Out*, 190.

3. Mark Deming, *Outsideinside* review, https://www.allmusic.com/album/outsideinside-mw0000525045.

4. Michael E. Tassone, conversation with author, January 4, 2023.

5. Steven Novak, phone call with author, January 20, 2023.

6. Edoardo Genzolini, *The Who: Concert Memories from the Classic Years, 1964–1976* (Atglen, PA: Schiffer, 2022), 70. See Craig Patterson's story on pages 136–138.

7. Pete's dialogue from Fillmore Auditorium, February 22, 1968 (Mark d'Ercole's recording, author's archive).

8. Andrew Neill and Matt Kent, *Anyway, Anyhow, Anywhere: The Complete Chronicle of the Who, 1958–1978* (London: Virgin Books, 2007), 197. See also Joe McMichael and "Irish" Jack Lyons, *The Who Concert File* (London: Omnibus Press, 2004), 97.

9. Bill Halverson, email sent to author, February 11, 2023.

10. Pete Townshend's interview and acoustic performance at the Free Library of Philadelphia, October 10, 2012, for the book launch of his autobiography *Who I Am*.

11. Pete's dialogue from Winterland, February 23, 1968, introducing the song "Tattoo" (Mark d'Ercole's tape, author's archive).

12. Richard Martin Frost, email sent to author, January 4, 2023; see also Genzolini, *The Who: Concert Memories from the Classic Years, 1964–1976*, 67.

13. James Terry Leary, *Who*??, message sent to author, March 3, 2023.

14. Michael Lazarus Scott, "Pete Gets Pissed," Facebook post from February 22, 2016.

15. JP Palmer, email sent to author, October 12, 2018.

Chapter 5. Winterland: Saturday, February 24, 1968; a Story in Photos

1. Anonymous source, message sent to author, June 6, 2022.

2. Find this story in Genzolini, *The Who: Concert Memories from the Classic Years, 1964–1976*, 55–56.

Chapter 6. The Years Between

1. Gilliland, Pop Chronicles Interviews #112—Pete Townshend, audio recording, February 5, 1968.

2. Neill and Kent, *Anyway, Anyhow, Anywhere: The Complete Chronicle of the Who, 1958–1978*, 192, 204; see also "Albums That Never Were: The Who—Who's For Tennis?," http://albumsthatneverwere.blogspot.com/2014/09/the-who-whos-for-tennis.html.

3. Pete's introduction to "I'm a Boy" at Winterland, February 23, 1968 (Mark D'Ercole's recording, author's archive).

4. Michael Geary, "An Interview with Roger Daltrey of The Who," *Informat*, in TN 131035: Jeep Holland Papers, 1943–1998, Bentley Historical Library, University of Michigan.

5. Pete Townshend claims the interview took place "at the home of Jack Casidy." *Pete Townshend, Who I Am* (London: HarperCollins, 2012), 148–149.

6. Genzolini, *The Who: Concert Memories from the Classic Years, 1964–1976*, 104. See Trisha Daly's letter to the Who Fan Club in London from August 16, 1968.

7. Rick M. Chapman, conversation with author, December 23, 2022.

8. Philip Elwood, "The Astounding Who: Perfection," *San Francisco Examiner*, June 15, 1970.

9. Nik Cohn, "Finally, the Full Force of the Who," *New York Times*, March 8, 1970.

10. Neill and Kent, *Anyway, Anyhow, Anywhere: The Complete Chronicle of the Who, 1958–1978*, 282.

11. Pat Lydon, "The Who: Its Pure Electric Energy Welds the Audience into a Cosmic Whole," *Boston Sunday Globe*, September 19, 1971.

12. Excerpt from a Chris Charlesworth interview featured inside the concert program, designed by Sorethroat Advertising, for the three nights at Boston Music Hall, August 4–6, 1971.

13. Lydon, "The Who: Its Pure Electric Energy Welds the Audience into a Cosmic Whole."

14. Ibid.

15. Chapman, *Meher Baba—the Compassionate One*, 23–25.

16. Townshend, *Who I Am*, 202–05.

17. Lydon, "The Who: Its Pure Electric Energy Welds the Audience into a Cosmic Whole."

18. "Now Pete's Brainchild Is Set for the Big Screen," unknown newspaper, in TN 131035: Jeep Holland Papers, 1943–1998, Bentley Historical Library, University of Michigan.

19. Chris Van Ness, "An Interview with Peter Townshend and the Who," unknown newspaper, in TN 131035: Jeep Holland Papers, 1943–1998, Bentley Historical Library, University of Michigan.

20. Ibid.

21. John L. Wasserman, "A Big Pounding by the Who," *San Francisco Examiner*, December 1971.

22. Lorenzo Filippo Giardina, "Leni Riefenstahl: Cinema di propaganda come trionfo del Reale," https://inchiostro.unipv.it/leni-riefenstahl-cinema-di-propaganda-come-trionfo-del-reale/.

Chapter 7. 1975–1976

1. "The Who Was in Danger of Becoming the Chuck Berrys of Sixties Rock. But I Think That Job Is Going to the Stones. Good luck," *Sounds*, April 5, 1975.

2. Nik Cohn, "Whoop-De-Do," unknown newspaper, December 15, 1975.

3. Ibid.

4. "The Who Was in Danger of Becoming the Chuck Berrys of Sixties Rock."

5. Roy Carr, "Pete Townshend: The Punk as Godfather—If the Glove Fits . . . ," *Creem*, September 1975.

6. Joel Selvin, *Altamont: The Rolling Stones, the Hells Angels, and the Inside Story of Rock's Darkest Day* (New York: Dey Street Books–HarperCollins, 2016), 139.

7. Anonymous source, message sent to author, January 7, 2023: sources from the underground scene state that the adding of strychnine to LSD is in fact a lie that was used back in the day to dissuade from taking acid.

8. Sam Cutler, *You Can't Always Get What You Want: My Life with the Rolling Stones, the Grateful Dead, and Other Wonderful Reprobates* (Toronto: ECW Press, 2010), 288–92.

9. Joe Taysom, "Jefferson Airplane's Grace Slick Allegedly Once Plotted to Spike President Nixon with LSD," *Far Out Magazine*, May 25, 2020, https://faroutmagazine.co.uk/jefferson-airplane-grace-slick-lsd-president-nixon-white-house/.

10. Mike Wiseman, conversation with author, January 6, 2023.

11. Chapman, *Bug Consciousness, Drug Consciousness, & Flying Rug Consciousness*, 72.

12. Genzolini, *The Who: Concert Memories from the Classic Years, 1964–1976*, 250, 290.

13. Fred Hauptfuhrer and Jim Jerome, "For Roger Daltrey, the Who Is No Longer the Question: It's Whether to Be a Star," *People*, December 15, 1975.

14. "The Who Was in Danger of Becoming the Chuck Berrys of Sixties Rock."

15. Hauptfuhrer and Jerome, "For Roger Daltrey, the Who Is No Longer the Question."

16. Gary Herman, "Who's Where in the Seventies?," *Let It Rock*, February 1975.

17. Tony Stewart, "Who's Last? Daltrey Fights Back," *Creem*, November 1975.

Chapter 8. San Francisco: March 27 and 28, 1976

1. Ralph J. Gleason, unknown title, *San Francisco Chronicle*, December 14, 1975.

2. Various authors, "The Who Could Have Sold 8 Times as Many," *San Francisco Examiner*, March 4, 1976.

3. Sansara-Nirvana Murphy, email sent to author, March 6, 2023.

Alterman, Loraine. "Just Be Patient! The Who Will Be Here." *Detroit Free Press*, April 7, 1967.

Carr, Roy. "Pete Townshend: The Punk as Godfather—If the Glove Fits . . ." *Creem*, September 1975.

Carr, Roy. "The Punk as Godfather II—If the Glove Fits . . . Wear It!" *Creem*, October 1975.

Chapman, Rick M. *Bug Consciousness, Drug Consciousness & Flying Rug Consciousness (the Dope on Drugs—Pot, Peyote, Acid, and Beyond—from the Source of Truth)*. Berkeley, CA: White Horse, 2022.

Chapman, Rick M. *Meher Baba—the Compassionate One*. Berkeley, CA: White Horse, 1987.

Cohn, Nik. "Finally, the Full Force of the Who." *New York Times*, March 8, 1970.

Cohn, Nik. "The Who: The Last of the Pop Groups." *Eye*, May 1968.

Cohn, Nik. "Whoop-De-Do." Unknown newspaper, December 15, 1975.

Cutler, Sam. *You Can't Always Get What You Want: My Life with the Rolling Stones, the Grateful Dead, and Other Wonderful Reprobates*. Toronto: ECW Press, 2010.

Darlington, Sandy. "Deaf, Dumb & Blind." *San Francisco Express Times*, August 21, 1968.

Deming, Mark. *Outsideinside* review. https://www.allmusic.com/album/outsideinside-mw0000525045.

Elwood, Philip. "The Astounding Who: Perfection." *San Francisco Examiner*, June 15, 1970.

Geary, Michael. "An Interview with Roger Daltrey of the Who." *Informat*, in TN 131035: Jeep Holland Papers, 1943–1998, Bentley Historical Library, University of Michigan.

Genzolini, Edoardo. *Cream: Clapton, Bruce & Baker Sitting on Top of the World, San Francisco, February–March 1968*. Atglen, PA: Schiffer, 2023.

Genzolini, Edoardo. *The Who: Concert Memories from the Classic Years, 1964–1976*. Atglen, PA: Schiffer, 2022.

Giardina, Lorenzo Filippo. "Leni Riefenstahl: Cinema di propaganda come trionfo del Reale." https://inchiostro.unipv.it/leni-riefenstahl-cinema-di-propaganda-come-trionfo-del-reale/.

Gilliland, John. Pop Chronicles Interviews #112—Pete Townshend, audio recording, February 5, 1968, https://digital.library.unt.edu/ark:/67531/metadc1692078/, accessed January 15, 2023, University of North Texas Libraries, UNT Digital Library, crediting UNT Music Library.

Gleason, Ralph J. Unknown title. *San Francisco Chronicle*, December 14, 1975.

Graham, Bill, and Robert Greenfield. *Bill Graham Presents: My Life inside Rock and Out*. Boston: Da Capo, 2004.

Hauptfuhrer, Fred, and Jim Jerome. "For Roger Daltrey, the Who Is No Longer the Question: It's Whether to Be a Star." *People*, December 15, 1975.

Herman, Gary. "Who's Where in the Seventies?" *Let It Rock*, February 1975.

Johnson, Jarid S. *This Old Building: The Closing of Winterland*. Photos by Jarid S. Johnson. Medford, OR: RRD | CDS, 2019.

Khan, Hazrat Inayat. *The Mysticism of Sound and Music*. Banff, AB: Ekstasis Editions, 2003.

Lopez, Sonya. "Who Is Tommy?" *2nd House*, BBC 2 Color, Saturday, October 5, 9:10 p.m., and *Who's Who*, Radio 1 Stereo, 2 p.m.

Lydon, Pat. "The Who: Its Pure Electric Energy Welds the Audience into a Cosmic Whole." *Boston Sunday Globe*, September 19, 1971.

Marcus, Greil. *Rock and Roll Will Stand*. Boston: Beacon Press, 1969.

Mark, Norman. "The Who Come Up with Pure Rock Opera." *San Francisco Examiner*, June 17, 1969.

Marshall, Ben, Pete Townshend, and Roger Daltrey. *The Who: The Official History*. London: Virgin, 2015.

McLuhan, Marshall. *Understanding Media: The Extensions of Man*. Cambridge, MA: MIT Press, 1994.

McMichael, Joe, and Jack Lyons. *The Who: Concert File*. London: Omnibus, 2004.

Meldahl, Nicole. "The Mysterious Death of the 'Mayor of the Fillmore.'" https://summerof.love/mysterious-death-mayor-fillmore/.

Neill, Andrew. *A Fortnight of Furore: The Who and the Small Faces Down Under*. London: Mutley, 1998.

Neill, Andrew, and Matt Kent. *Anyway, Anyhow, Anywhere: The Complete Chronicle of the Who, 1958–1978*. London: Virgin Books, 2007.

Ngā Taonga Sound & Vision. *Peter Townshend*. RNZ collection, ID25183.

"Now Pete's Brainchild Is Set for the Big Screen." Unknown newspaper, in TN 131035: Jeep Holland Papers, 1943–1998, Bentley Historical Library, University of Michigan.

Palmer, Tony. *Born under a Bad Sign*. London: HarperCollins, 1970.

Pepin, Elizabet, and Lewis Watts. *Harlem of the West: The San Francisco Fillmore Jazz Era*. San Francisco: Chronicle, 2005.

Roth, Molly. "Break-Up Artists Smashing Success." *Shamokin News Dispatch*, January 6, 1968.

Selvin, Joel. *Altamont: The Rolling Stones, the Hells Angels, and the Inside Story of Rock's Darkest Day*. New York: Dey Street Books–HarperCollins, 2016.

Selvin, Joel. *The Haight: Love, Rock, and Revolution; The Photography of Jim Marshall*. San Francisco: Insight, 2014.

Selvin, Joel. *Summer of Love: The Inside Story of LSD, Rock & Roll, Free Love, and High Times in the Wild West*. New York: E. P. Dutton, 1994.

Smith, Kenneth. *Émile Durkheim and the Collective Consciousness of Society: A Study in Criminology*. New York: Anthem, 2014.

Sorethroat Advertising, Boston Music Hall, August 4–6, 1971, concert program.

Stein, Bruno. "Roger Daltrey: Talkin' Bout My D-D-Dedication." *Creem*, January 1975.

Stewart, Tony. "Who's Last? Daltrey Fights Back." *Creem*, November 1975.

Taysom, Joe. "Jefferson Airplane's Grace Slick Allegedly Once Plotted to Spike President Nixon with LSD." *Far Out Magazine*, May 25, 2020. https://faroutmagazine.co.uk/jefferson-airplane-grace-slick-lsd-president-nixon-white-house/.

Townshend, Pete. *Who I Am*. London: HarperCollins, 2012.

Townshend, Pete, and Jeff Young. *Lifehouse: Adapted for Radio by Jeff Young*. London: Pocket, 1999.

Van Ness, Chris. "An Interview with Peter Townshend and the Who." Unknown newspaper, in TN 131035: Jeep Holland Papers, 1943–1998, Bentley Historical Library, University of Michigan.

Various authors. "Regina to Get Look at 'Turned-On' Who." *Leader Post* (Regina, SK), June 29, 1968.

Various authors. "The Who Could Have Sold 8 Times as Many." *San Francisco Examiner*, March 4, 1976.

VJEOW, Dutch TV. John Peel interviews Pete Townshend, October 30, 1967.

Wasserman, John L. "A Big Pounding by the Who." *San Francisco Examiner*, December 1971.

Wenner, Jann. "The Rolling Stone Interview: Peter Townshend." *Rolling Stone* 17–18 (September 18 and 24, 1968).

"The Who Was in Danger of Becoming the Chuck Berrys of Sixties Rock. But I Think That Job Is Going to the Stones. Good Luck." *Sounds*, April 5, 1975.